AMAZED
by the POWER
of GOD

Amazed by the Power of God

⌘

Contributors

Bill Johnson

Randy Clark

Carol and Christy Wimber

S.J. Hill

Bobby Conner

Doug Addison

David Tomberlin

Charles H. Kraft

Marcus Lawson

Denny Cline

Peter H. Davids

Gary Best

⌘

Compiler

Frank A. DeCenso Jr.

DESTINY IMAGE PUBLISHERS

BILL JOHNSON · RANDY CLARK
CAROL & CHRISTY WIMBER · S.J. HILL
BOBBY CONNER · DOUG ADDISON
DAVID TOMBERLIN · CHARLES H. KRAFT
MARC LAWSON · DENNY CLINE
PETER H. DAVIDS · GARY BEST

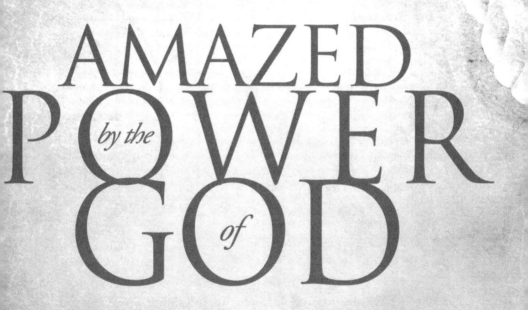

AMAZED
P*by the*WER
G*of*OD

COMPILED BY
FRANK DeCENSO JR.

DESTINY IMAGE® PUBLISHERS, INC.

P.O. Box 310, Shippensburg, PA 17257-0310

"Speaking to the Purposes of God for this Generation and for the Generations to Come."

This book and all other Destiny Image, Revival Press, Mercy Place, Fresh Bread, Destiny Image Fiction, and Treasure House books are available at Christian bookstores and distributors worldwide.

For a U.S. bookstore nearest you, call 1-800-722-6774.

For more information on foreign distributors, call 717-532-3040.

Reach us on the Internet at www.destinyimage.com.

ISBN 10: 0-7684-2755-X   ISBN 13: 978-0-7684-2755-4

For Worldwide Distribution, Printed in the U.S.A.

1 2 3 4 5 6 7 8 9 10 11 / 13 12 11 10 09

Contents

The only book that should ever be written is one that flows up from the heart, forced out by the inward pressure. When such a work has gestated within a man, it is almost certain that it will be written. The man who is thus charged with a message will not be turned back by any blasé consideration. His book will be to him not only imperative, it will be inevitable.

—A.W. TOZER, *God's Pursuit of Man*

HEARING GOD

For some, hearing God is an art. For others, hearing God speak can be a surprise. I am convinced by events in my life that God enjoys surprising me by speaking to me when I am engaged in the most rudimentary of tasks, like driving or showering.

Not long ago after showering, an interesting "thought" popped into my head: *Assemble a group of people to write a book about the relevance of My power in today's world.* The thought caught me off guard; although it came in a millisecond, I immediately understood what it entailed. But to be honest, I didn't know how it would all come together. After praying and sending out numerous requests to people whom I knew to be involved in power ministry, I received an overwhelmingly positive response. At one point there were almost 60 people who were interested in contributing to a book or series of books about the power of God today.

Armed with credible contributors, I sent out a few feelers to find out if anyone would be interested in publishing such a compendium by authors, ministers, and scholars. Destiny Image expressed interest, and you have in your hands a piece of that original mandate from God.

I'm convinced that God wants His children to catch the vision of moving in His power to change other's lives and to tell all people that He is in love with them. He can do it through subtle ways, but the church needs to be equipped so that He can move mightily through us in today's world. The healing of cancer or deliverance from addiction can do more than any apologetic argument, because the affected one will have been personally touched by the living, loving God of the universe. His power is more effective than our words.

WHO CAN MOVE IN THE POWER OF GOD?

Peter was a fisherman. And John at one time wanted to keep folks who weren't following Jesus from casting out demons, and he also wanted to cast fire down from Heaven on those who did not receive Jesus. Later these men both received power from on high by encountering God powerfully and personally, to do works of ministry. They were used to heal a man, and the religious folks got upset. In fact the Pharisees said that Peter and John were "untrained and uneducated," but even so, there was no denying that they had been with Jesus. That's what accredits people for ministry—being with Jesus, partnering with Jesus, loving Him more than any scholastic endeavor or miraculous event.

But "professional ministers" can't change the world alone. The church needs ordinary people willing to minister wherever they are, because lives need to be changed, the sick need to be healed, and the oppressed need to be delivered. This will happen through "ordinary Christians" who want to bring God's Kingdom to others through the means and giftings they have received.

God is not interested in humankind's wisdom. He's interested in our obedience to be used as conduits of His power to change lives. Counseling from a textbook isn't going to deliver someone oppressed by demons. God's power will. And He can use anyone at anytime—we just need to be willing to be used.

John Wimber, the late leader of the Vineyard Movement, taught that in church everyone gets to play. He taught people how to move in the Spirit—not because he learned it in seminary, but because Jesus taught and showed him personally. We need thousands more like Wimber who can reach the average Joes and Janes who walk into a church the day after becoming a Christian and ask, "What's this Christianity about?" If we say, "It's about listening to Dr. Pastor Jones articulate a well-exegeted sermon on the dietary laws' applicability today," boy, we're all in big trouble.

But if we say, "Come on in! Christianity is about loving God and learning to hear His voice so you can tell your friends and relatives and neighbors about Jesus, *and* show them in power how much Jesus loves them," *then* the world will be radically reached and impacted.

PURPOSE

It's my firm belief that a revolution of power-enhanced ministers will emerge from the grassroots level—believers tired of "Churchianity" and pew-warming. Part of my goal in life is to equip the saints in the church to do ministry. Ministry isn't just for professionals who can speak Latin. It's for everyone who can hear God's heartbeat for a lost and dying world, and respond with clarity and take risks that can make a positive difference.

It's my hope that this book will persuade and equip Christians of several generations that God is in the power business—not to show off, but to bless, encourage, and heal hurting lives. He cared enough to send Jesus to die on the cross; He also cares enough to move today in power.

Chapter 1

INHERITING THE SUPERNATURAL

❦

BILL JOHNSON

Bill and Brenda (Beni) Johnson are senior pastors of Bethel Church in Redding, California. Bill is a fifth generation pastor with a rich heritage in the things of the Spirit. Together they serve a growing number of churches that have partnered for revival. This apostolic network has crossed denominational lines in building relationships that enable church leaders to walk in both purity and power.

The Lord has used Bill to launch a frontal attack against unbelief, complacency, and doubt. Through healings that occur at every meeting, faith has been strengthened and revival fires fanned in the hearts of believers. Bill teaches a life of faith that produces a relationship between the Faithful One and the surrendered believer. The power of God reveals His nature and is ushered in by His Presence. Bill believes that teaching truths about God without an encounter leads to spiritual pride. An encounter with God produces both a revelation of God and revelation of self, thus transforming us.

In this present move, God has brought Bill into a deeper understanding of the phrase, "...on earth as it is in heaven." Heaven is the model for our life and ministry. Jesus lived with this principle by only doing what He saw His Father doing. Learning to recognize the Holy Spirit's presence and how to follow His lead enables us to do the works of Christ—destroying the works of the devil. Healing and deliverance must become the common expression of the gospel of power once again.

Bill and the Bethel church family have taken on this theme for life and ministry. Healings, ranging from cancer to broken bones to learning disorders and emotional healing, happen with regularity. This is the "children's bread." And these works of God are not limited to revival meetings. The church is learning how to take this anointing to the schools, workplace, and neighborhoods with similar results. Bill teaches that we owe the world an encounter with God, and that the gospel without power is not the gospel that Jesus preached.

Bill's reflection about the power of God follows:

JESUS CHRIST IS PERFECT THEOLOGY

Jesus Christ is perfect theology. Whatever you think you know about God that you can't find in the person of Jesus, you have a reason to question. Jesus Christ is the precise revelation of the nature of the Father. As Jesus is manifested to us in Scripture, so we are to present Him to this world. Revelation makes us responsible and accountable, for He said to us, "As the Father has sent Me, I also send you" (John 20:21).

Early in life through the Christmas message we hear the angels proclaim, "Glory to God in the highest, and on earth peace, *goodwill toward men!*" (Luke 2:14). This is God's heart toward humanity. It's the message that introduced Jesus to the world and must remain the message that introduces the Church to the world.

Believers easily say, "Yes, God is good." We have to; the Bible says so. But when tragedy strikes, many say, "I know He's good, but His ways are mysterious," thinking that God causes evil because He'll work it out for good in the end. The implication is that God sometimes brings crises, disease, and torment to teach us to be better Christians. There is no question that God can work good out of evil. This is a testimony to His greatness, and His redemptive purpose in our lives. But to attribute evil to Him tragically undermines our purpose on the earth, as it cripples our ability to *re*-present Jesus as the manifestation of God's *goodwill toward all*. Furthermore it compromises our ability to discern the difference between God's discipline and actual demonic assault.

Conflict often arises when discussing the nature of God's goodness. The portrayal of God "as one who afflicts" usually has an old covenant Scripture as its proof text. It is wrong to take an Old Testament revelation of God, of His nature, and preempt or trump the New Testament revelation of God found in Jesus Christ. Inferior covenants do not provide clearer insights into the nature of God.

Scripture is Scripture. All of it was written for our instruction. But what is observed in the Law and the Prophets does not possess the clarity that is found in the person of Jesus.

PURPOSE FOR THE OLD TESTAMENT

There are countless benefits of the Old Testament Scriptures for the New Testament believer. But improper use of them has impaired many a Christian's life. Here are at least three beneficial uses.

1. The Old Testament gives us an awareness of our sinfulness. The apostle Paul explains it, "...where there is no law there is no transgression" (Rom. 4:15).

2. The Old Testament Law is the tutor that leads us to Christ. "Therefore the Law has become our *tutor* to lead us to Christ, so that we may be justified by faith. But now that faith has come, we are no longer under a *tutor*" (Gal. 3:24-25 NASB).

3. In that the Old Testament leads us to Jesus, it naturally portrays this King in His Kingdom. Throughout the time before Christ, there were events, prophecies, and laws that spoke of life under grace. There were unusual moments of grace that gave insight into what was coming through "types and shadows."

Wonderful revelations are gained from the Old Testament through types and shadows. For example, we know that the Jews sacrificed a spotless lamb at the temple as a payment for their sin. But we also know that Jesus is the actual Lamb of God who takes away the sin of the world. Once fulfillment comes to the Old

Testament type or symbol, there's no more need to go back and embrace the shadow.

The new covenant reveals the Father clearly in the person of Jesus Christ. Jesus said, "If you've seen Me, you've seen the Father" (see John 14:9). Hebrews declares, "God, after He spoke long ago to the fathers in the prophets in many portions and in many ways, in these last days has spoken to us in His Son" (Heb. 1:1-2 NASB). Furthermore, He is "the exact representation of His nature." God is now speaking primarily through the person and work of Jesus. The two are exactly alike. That is what is so *new* about the New Testament—God is seen clearly in Jesus.

The entire Old Testament points to Jesus. He is the central figure of Scripture. The Law and the Prophets declare His role as Messiah and assure us that Jesus is the One—the fulfillment of God's redemptive plan. The stories, prophecies, and laws all point to Him at various levels in the same way a highway sign points to an upcoming city. The sign is real and significant. But in itself it is not the reality we are looking for. It points to something greater than itself. In this case we must not worship the sign of the Old Testament. It serves its purpose by taking us to the Messiah Himself. A freeway sign never defines the city itself, and neither should the Old Testament redefine who Jesus is. He is the fulfillment of both the Law and the Prophets. The nature of His life and purpose is clear— He came to *destroy* the works of the devil.

There is a deep personal need in the Body of Christ to see Jesus for who He is. Jesus healed everyone who came to Him. That doesn't change because not everyone I pray for gets healed. He stilled every life-threatening storm that He encountered. And deliverance came to all who asked. This is Jesus. And this is the Father, exactly.

There is a vast difference between the goodness of God seen in the life of Jesus and the goodness of God revealed in the Church because of our present-day beliefs. It has become easier to believe either that the standard Jesus set for our lives is entirely unattainable or that it is theologically wrong to consider it a legitimate standard for today. It is far too difficult for many to reconcile the differences in the life of Jesus and the experience of the everyday believer; so bad theology is created. It's sometimes easier to change our interpretation of the intent of Scripture than it is to seek God until He answers.

If Jesus healed everyone who came to Him, and the Father wills people to be sick, then we have a divided house—one that according to Jesus cannot stand. Invariably it's at this point in the discussion that people bring up Old Testament verses in an attempt to prove the point that God causes sickness. I can't think of an area other than miracles, signs, and wonders, which would include prophecy, that the Church does this with. We would never endorse the sacrifice of an actual lamb to atone for sin even though the Old Testament gave the command. Nor would we make people travel to Jerusalem so they can be involved in acceptable worship to God. These things we would never do. But we do the equivalent to the subject of healing. If an Old Testament Scripture supersedes the perfect revelation of God in Christ on the subject of healing, we have illegally taken license to redefine the nature of the Kingdom. We do this with no other part of the gospel.

Two thousand years ago Jesus considered all sickness to be from the devil, and healing was a sign of God's Kingdom come. Even something as simple as a fever was considered to be of the devil. (See Mark 1:31.) Things have disintegrated so far that many consider sickness to be sent or allowed by God to build our character. Those who pursue healing are thought to be out of balance at best, and from the devil at worst. It's frightening to see how far things can fall in 2,000 years. What is even more puzzling is that the very ones who consider the sickness to be approved by God for our benefit have no problem going to the doctor to find a cure and release from disease. Such mindless approaches to Scripture must stop.

Believing that God is good is absolutely vital to becoming effective in the ministry of the gospel. Without that foundation, it's not possible to develop the clear focus and the strength of faith to pursue the breakthroughs that the earth aches for. The way we understand Him *is* the way we will present Him. How we see Him defines how we think and how we live.

I am not saying that God doesn't discipline. When I talk about the goodness of God and the greatness of Jesus and His grace and His kindness, I don't forget that He was also the one who chased the moneychangers out of the temple with a whip. It's just that He does not use sickness, any more than He uses sin, to discipline His children. If I did to my children what many Christians claim God does to His, I'd be arrested for child abuse.

When we understand the nature of God, we see that Jesus is not warring against the Father to reveal a different standard. He is perfectly representing and manifesting the nature of the Father. This is a big deal because in the back of the minds of so many people is a picture of the Father willing certain calamities and difficulties and Jesus interceding, trying to talk Him out of it. While very few will put it in that language, it is the imagery that is behind much of how the Church lives and thinks. Insurance companies and newspapers call natural disasters "an act of God." Where did they get their theology? From us.

We don't ever find Jesus blessing a storm that was coming at Him and the disciples. He never redirected the storm, saying, "Go to that city; destroy them. It will teach them how to pray. They will become more like Me." On the contrary, He stilled the storm. He rebuked His disciples for wanting to call down fire on people, saying, "You don't know what spirit you are of." (See Luke 9:54.) We never see Him using His authority to increase a storm or to bring calamity of any kind. We always see Him bringing an end to a storm or sickness. Regardless of how or why the storm came about, Jesus was the solution.

We can either create a doctrine that allows for lack, or seek God until He answers. When the disciples didn't get a miracle breakthrough, they asked Jesus why. In other words, they expected breakthrough. An environment of expectation naturally creates a desire to find out "why" when a breakthrough doesn't come. Today it's easier to blame God than to accept the fact that we're the ones He left in charge.

THE NATURE OF THE MESSAGE

"The Law and the Prophets were proclaimed until John; since that time the gospel of the kingdom of God has been preached, and everyone is forcing his way into it" (Luke 16:16 NASB).

"Until John" is a significant phrase, but one that is nearly forgotten. Both the Law and the Prophets were superseded by another message, the gospel of the Kingdom. One still exists; the other has become obsolete. One has Heaven's backing; the other doesn't. One reveals our assignment; the other does not.

A message creates a reality. The nature of the message determines the nature of the reality in which we will live and minister. The Kingdom message creates an environment suitable to the display of God's love, purity, and power. It is the message that Jesus preached and in turn taught His disciples to preach. It is the *now word*.

The Church has largely replaced the gospel of the Kingdom with the gospel of salvation. The gospel of salvation is focused on getting people saved and going to Heaven. The beauty of that message makes it very easy to miss the fact that it is only a part of the whole message that Jesus gave us. The gospel of the Kingdom is focused on the transformation of lives, cities, and nations, bringing the reality of Heaven to earth. We must not confuse our destiny with our assignment. *Heaven is my destiny, while bringing the Kingdom is my assignment.* The focus of the Kingdom message is the rightful dominion of God over everything.

Whatever is inconsistent with Heaven, namely disease, torment, sin habits, etc., must come under the authority of the King. These kinds of issues must be dealt with and broken off of people's lives because these inferior realms cannot stand wherever the dominion of God is realized. As we succeed in displaying this message, we are positioned to bring about cultural change in business, politics, the environment, and essential issues that face us today. This creates a most unusual phenomenon: the fruit of revival becomes the fuel of revival, which produces the fruit of revival, etc. It is circular, unto reformation.

WHEN HEAVEN WAS SILENT

Why did Jesus say, "until John"? Why didn't He say, "until Jesus"? Because John was the one who broke Heaven's silence with the message of the Kingdom. Before John the Baptist came on the scene, there were 400 years without one word from God. Heaven was silent. No visions, dreams, or prophecies. Nothing. Four hundred years of absolute silence, and then came John. The Holy Spirit is not carelessly highlighting this detail that the Law and the Prophets were until John because it was John who first declared, "Repent, for the Kingdom of Heaven is at hand" (Matt. 3:2).

There is another place in Scripture where 400 years is unusually significant. Understanding the first mention of this phrase, *400 years*, will help us to understand its significance in this case. Israel was a nation of slaves, living in Egypt for 400 years. And then everything changed in a moment. The blood from a lamb was put on the doorpost of each Jewish home on the Passover (see Exod. 12:23). The Angel of the Lord came and released the Jews from their slavery to Egypt. In one moment, they went from being slaves, to being free, from absolute poverty, to possessing the wealth of the most prosperous nation in the world. It happened in a moment. The first mention of the phrase *400 years* in the Bible resulted in the rescue and creation of a new nation, the redemption of God's people. In the time of John, God announces a rescue and creation of a new nation declaring, "It's a new day!"

That is exactly the message of Jesus in Luke 16:16. It's a new day! The new day is marked with a new message. One message is over, and another has begun. When John the Baptist came forth, it was even more significant than deliverance from 400 years of slavery under Egypt. This deliverance dealt with the nature and potential of humankind. John's pronouncement changed everything.

Jesus made the amazing statement, "Now the Kingdom of God is being preached and *everyone is pressing into it*" (see Luke 16:16). Is it possible that the nature of the message determines the size of the harvest? He did say, *everyone!* This is the message: "Jesus is Lord over all. His dominion is everlasting. It is *now!*" When you declare the right message, you create an atmosphere where everyone is able to press in. No matter the need, there is an answer. The right message capitalizes on the truth that Jesus is called *The Desire of the Nations.* The right message changes the atmosphere to make the manifestation of His dominion realized. Perhaps this is the context in which the irresistible grace of God is embraced, thus fulfilling the desire born in the heart of every person alive.

IT IS FINISHED

> *After this, Jesus, knowing that all things were now accomplished, that the Scripture might be fulfilled, said, "I thirst!" ... So when Jesus had received the sour wine, He said, **"It is finished!"** And bowing His head, He gave up His spirit* (John 19:28,30).

It is a mistake to think that when Jesus cried out, "It is finished," He was merely proclaiming that His life as a human being was over. He came to quench the appetite of an unquenchable fire by satisfying the demands of the Law and the Prophets. When He said, "It is finished," He was declaring, "The appetite of the Law and

Prophets has been satisfied. It's a new day. It is finished." We go from a slave to a possessor of the Kingdom in a moment: from being the one who has no right in God to suddenly being the eternal dwelling place of God Himself.

REPENTING ENOUGH TO SEE THE KINGDOM

"Repent, for the Kingdom of Heaven is at hand." One of the ways I like to illustrate this is in Hebrews 6:1, "Repentance *from* dead works…faith *toward* God." Full repentance is *from* something *toward* something—*from* sin *toward* God. Many Christians repent enough to be forgiven but not enough to see the Kingdom. Their repentance doesn't bring the Kingdom into view. Jesus tells us to repent because He brought His world with Him. If I don't shift my perspective on reality, I will never discover that which is superior—the unseen realm of His dominion.

Luke writes it this way: "Repent therefore and be converted, that your sins may be blotted out, so that times of refreshing may come from the presence of the Lord" (Acts 3:19). The point is: *the presence is the Kingdom.* It's too easy to over-complicate the Christian life. We are told to put on the full armor of God, which includes the helmet of salvation, breastplate of righteousness, and so on (see Eph. 6:10-18). The apostle Paul gave us this important instruction, but most of us miss the point. God *is* my armor. He's not saying, "Put something on that is a reality that is separate from Me." He's saying, "I'm it. Just abide in Me. I become your salvation. I am your righteousness, the breastplate over you. I am the gospel of peace. I am the good news. I am the sword of the Spirit." This list is a profound word picture enabling us to realize the fuller benefit of abiding in Christ.

The Kingdom is about discovering presence, the person of the Lord Jesus Christ. Why? He's the message. He's perfect theology. We can't defile or distort the message of who He is so that we can accommodate something that took place in the days of an inferior covenant. To try to reactivate the voice of the Law and Prophets, and let it trump and overtake the clear manifestation of the nature of God found in Jesus, is theologically immoral.

RELEASING HIS PRESENCE

Remember when Jesus sent the disciples out two by two? He told them to go into a home, let their peace rest on that home, and if there was not a person of peace there, they should take the peace back and leave. (See Luke 10:5-7.) That was vital ministry instruction that most of us know little about. In order to understand this issue, we need a stronger awareness of our relationship with the Holy Spirit.

There is an Old Testament type and shadow of the Holy Spirit descending as a dove in the story of Noah. He released the dove to find out if there was any dry land. When the dove could find no place to rest, the dove returned to Noah. Every time you talk and you declare Kingdom realities, you release the Holy Spirit. And He is looking for a life to rest upon. Learning how that presence is released is essential in ministry. I find that the same thing happens when we are with people who have a genuine hunger for the Kingdom. They actually draw upon the Spirit within us. That is how Jesus knew that power went out from Him when the woman touched the edge of His garment (see Mark 5:30). He carried such an awareness of the Holy Spirit upon Him that He felt power being released.

As we speak, His presence is released. He is always looking for another person to rest upon. This is their call and summons into their eternal purpose as the dwelling place of God, and as a broker of His dominion. When we talk about the Kingdom of God being at hand, we are talking about the presence of the Almighty God. You cannot separate presence and Kingdom.

Our ministry *is* the release of presence. It is why we say what He is saying because as we speak, our words define the ministry of the Spirit of God that is being released and manifested into the environment. We are called and assigned by God to stand within society and bring the Word of the Lord. We are even told of a day coming when the nations of the world will stream to us seeking the word of the Lord (see Micah 4:2).

A WORD BORN IN COURAGE

An expression of the *dunamis* power released on the Church at Pentecost is courage. Courage enables us to speak with a boldness that God says "Amen" to. Declaring His word requires courage. And manifesting His will is our intentional response to the word we just declared that requires risk. Much of what is preached today is without boldness. If Jesus had preached what was preached in most pulpits on any given Sunday, He never would have been crucified.

"And they went out and preached everywhere, the Lord working with them, confirming the word through the accompanying signs" (Mark 16:19). Much of what is presently taught and confessed by the Church can be accomplished apart from God. Most of it appeals to human talent and skill. Whatever we can do for God is important but secondary to what we've been called to do that is impossible. The ability to rally the people of God together and work hard to accomplish a project for the Lord will never satisfy our inner longing to see impossibilities bend their knee to the name of Jesus.

But the Lord is stirring up a courage that is anchored to eternal purpose. In Acts 4:29-30, Peter had just gotten out of prison; he had just suffered persecution for the name of Jesus, yet he was ready to take it up a notch. He said, "Lord, please take note of their threats and grant that Your bondservants could preach Your word with all boldness." He asked God to increase his boldness: the very thing that got him in trouble. The Lord is looking for a word that is born in courage, so that He *has* to show up to confirm it. May the Lord give us a word that confronts the powers of darkness, releases Heaven on earth, and launches people into their God-born destinies: something to which God can say "Amen."

We are a people chosen by God to declare what God is saying, releasing the presence of the Lord all over the earth. This was all His idea—that the glory of the Lord would cover the earth as the water covers the sea, and there would be no end to the increase of His government. You and I are servants in bringing the kingdoms of this world into His domain, where the presence of God is seen in every aspect and area of life.

THE POWER OF RIGHTEOUSNESS

Societal transformation is not an accidental by-product of revival. It is to be intentional. In revival the Church becomes more convinced of a big God than a big devil. Such a shift in focus changes what's possible. But it's our internal world that is the first thing to change in the glory of His outpouring. For such a transformation to take place in the world around us, it must first happen to the world within us. Only what is true on the inside can be released to the outside. Jesus conquered a storm with peace. It was the storm He slept in. The peace that kept Him in rest was the peace that delivered Him from the storm itself. Internal realities become our external realities. That is the nature of ministry: living from the inside out.

Without the outpouring of the Spirit, the Church becomes more concerned with being contaminated by evil than we do of contaminating the world with righteousness. While we should never take sin lightly, neither should we be ignorant of the power of holiness.

Much of our present view of the world is built on Old Testament revelation. It's not wrong; it's just incomplete. If I lived under Jewish law before Christ, and I offered a sacrifice to the Lord, but on the way to the temple someone who was unclean touched my offering, the offering would have become unclean. Sin affects. That's why touching a leper made a person unclean. The emphasis in the old covenant revelation was that sin is powerful. It destroys whatever it touches.

Things are different in the New Testament. The Gospel of Matthew was written primarily for the Jews. In his account of Jesus' life, Matthew mentioned Jesus touching the leper as the first miracle. When He touched the leper, the leper became clean. This testimony confronted an incomplete mindset that was not adequate for His present work of grace on the earth. The power of holiness becomes even clearer when we read that a believing spouse sanctifies the entire unbelieving household. This Kingdom mindset requires a shift in how we view and value life itself and the effect of the life of Christ in us. Faith in Kingdom realities manifests Kingdom realities.

The power of holiness becomes clearer in the story of Daniel. God took Daniel and allowed him to be numbered with witches and warlocks before King Nebuchadnezzar. He lived righteously and brought about a New Testament effect of holiness and loyalty on an entire kingdom until that ungodly leader was converted. Holiness is more powerful than sin; it's the purity of Christ in you.

HIGHWAY OF HOLINESS

There is an environment created in the outpouring of the Spirit where holiness becomes the natural by-product. Isaiah speaks of the highway of holiness. A highway is a road designed to expedite travel, where obstacles have been removed. It usually involves easy access and fellow travelers. A highway of holiness builds momentum for the people of God to live in purity. It is so significant that even foolish things get covered. It's not to call for, allow for, or encourage foolish things. Many living righteously create a momentum where even the weak succeed.

A highway shall be there, and a road,
And it shall be called the Highway of Holiness.
The unclean shall not pass over it,
But it shall be for others.
Whoever walks the road, although a fool,
Shall not go astray (Isaiah 35:8).

This Highway of Holiness will not be known for compromise. You won't have people who outwardly pretend to be holy but inwardly are corrupt. "Whoever walks the road, although a fool, shall not go astray" means that God is creating such a highway in this time of outpouring that it's going to be hard to wander off the road. This concept is difficult for many to receive as we are accustomed to the opposite. We are quick to speak about the "great falling away," but not the great harvest and city transformation that is also a part of end-time prophecy. A day is coming when there will exist a righteous peer pressure, without the fear of man.

New Testament theology emphasizes the power of holiness, not the power of sin. It's not that we shouldn't fear sin. It remains powerful. But a shift in focus will position us to invade the world instead of requiring the world to come to us.

I remember being taught that holiness was a list of things you can and can't do—and the "can't do" list was longer than the "can do" list. Mostly what was on the can do list was go to Church, tithe, give offerings, witness, read your Bible, and pray. Throw in a potluck now and then, have a good life, and wait until Jesus comes back. But Jesus didn't go through all that He went through so we could be busy with religious activities. He placed the Spirit of resurrection within us that we might conquer something.

Most have an Old Testament view of holiness in a New Testament era—and the eras are completely different. The Old Testament was to prepare humanity for a Savior—not just to prepare them to receive one, but to prepare them to ask for one. The Law and the

Prophets continually exposed requirements from God that people could not keep. But grace came along and changed everything. You can't do enough stuff to make yourself clean before God. We are in desperate need of a Savior and even now, 2,000 years later, it is vital we live with that consciousness—that we cannot work hard enough to get God's favor. We have His favor, and we must live from that favor to increase what we already have.

It's a strange concept in the Kingdom. You actually get more of what you have by living out of what you have. If you can make that adjustment and learn to live in grace, your conduct changes so much more dramatically than when you try to work to obtain favor.

The prophet Isaiah continues this most beautiful picture of a highway concept.

> *Go through, go through the gates,*
> *Clear the way for the people;*
> *Build up,*
> *Build up the highway,*
> *Remove the stones,*
> *Lift up a standard over the peoples* (Isaiah 62:10 NASB).

I believe the gates in this passage refer to *praise,* as mentioned in Isaiah 60:18. When the people of God give God praise, something happens in the atmosphere. The obstacles of ideologies, culture, and spiritual strongholds are confronted. Continuous praise, that is both sacrificial, and a lifestyle, eventually removes the inferior and establishes a Heaven-like realm over geographical locations. It happens wherever the people of God gather to worship, but eventually it has an effect on entire cities. This heavenly atmosphere changes people's perception of reality. This process is called building a highway. A worshiping community changes the atmosphere over the city that actually gives those who don't know Christ a place of easy access to know Him.

HOLINESS MANIFESTS IN POWER

Holiness in character is the manifestation of the power of God on the nature of man. Holiness affects the human body through healing. Holiness demands expression, and that expression is the manifestation of power, giving language to what the Spirit of God is doing. The Lord was "declared to be the Son of God with power according to the Spirit of holiness by the resurrection of the dead" (Rom. 1:4). Miracles, like the resurrection, are a normal expression of holiness.

At times our love for God is measured by that which we hate. He is still the judge and will always condemn whatever interferes with love. How much did God hate sickness? As much as He hated sin. They are dealt with almost as one and the same. What sin is to my soul, sickness is to my body. He hated sickness enough to allow His Son to experience such a brutal whipping. The blood covers our sin, but the wounds paid for our miracle. That is how much He hates sin *and* sickness. We cannot be tolerant of those things, because what you tolerate dominates.

OUR COMMISSION

Holiness has a transforming effect on all creation as well. Romans 8:22 says that "creation groans for the revealing of the sons and daughters of God." Nature longs to manifest the Kingdom. The earth groans for this, wanting to be healed. Even water longs to be walked on again. While I'm not contending for our trying to create an earthly utopia, I am also not discounting the fact that creation is affected by the manifestation of God's presence upon His people.

What happens in the spirit needs to be measurable in the natural. If you say you love God whom you can't see and you hate your brother whom you can see, then what you are saying is a lie about your love for God (see 1 John 4:20). In other words, what you claim to experience in the unseen realm has to be able to be manifested in the seen realm, or what you claim is in question. He won't let us live with theories that cannot be tested. They've got to be applicable now.

The prophets used natural language to teach of spiritual realities. The desert rejoices in Isaiah 35:1. In verse 2, it blossoms abundantly with joy and singing and the glory of the Lord will be seen. Verses 3 and 4 are the commission: "Strengthen weak hands. Make firm feeble knees. Say to those who are fearful hearted, 'Be strong. Do not fear. Your God will come with vengeance.'"

Run and look for anyone who's faltering and say, "This isn't the time to falter. This is our moment, the moment you were born for. Don't be afraid." Having the right message in the right hour releases an unparalleled realm of supernatural activity. This is Heaven's response to our response to His commission: "Then the eyes of the blind shall be opened and the ears of the deaf shall be unstopped. The lame shall leap like the deer, and the tongue of the dumb shall sing" (Isa. 35:5-6). This is God's "Amen" to our proclaiming the right message. And he uses nature to illustrate the abundant Christian life: "For waters will burst forth in the wilderness, and streams in the desert...."

A DRINK BECOMES A RIVER

Jesus became sin so that you and I would become the righteousness of God. We became God's righteousness in the earth. He says, "Arise, shine for His light has come," not "Arise and *reflect*"— because once you are touched by light, you *become* light. He says that if we come to Him and drink, out of our innermost being will flow rivers of living water (see John 7:38). So a drink of Him turns your innermost being into a producer of a river whose volume is so much greater than the drink you received. You become a releaser of that very Kingdom that impacted and changed you. Your nature, your being, your person, everything about you, is dramatically shifted in the moment you come into contact with the King and His Kingdom.

The Kingdom culture celebrates what God is doing without stumbling over what God didn't do. We must resist the temptation to build our theology around what didn't happen. The world around us cries for an authentic display of Christ. And we become that answer if we don't stumble over what didn't happen.

We are responsible to seek Him for specific breakthrough in private. Also learn from those who have already experienced the breakthrough you long for. Being in the environment of their ministry releases a grace to do the same. Be ready to receive from those who are outside of your theological preferences, as God often hides His best gifts for us in the most unlikely package, just to ensure we have the necessary hunger and humility to live in the gift once we receive it. Look for the impossible and take the risks necessary to confront it and give opportunity for a miracle.

May God release a Spirit of wisdom and revelation upon His people once again that we might see Jesus more clearly, and that we might *re*-present Jesus more accurately. In the same way that Moses' face shone with the glory of God after seeing His unlimited goodness, so God wants to change the face of the Church in our generation.

The goodness of God is the cornerstone of our theology: one that must be lived, preached, and demonstrated.

It's all about Jesus, who is perfect theology.

Chapter 2

CHRISTIANITY'S GREAT HEALING RIVER AND ITS CONTRIBUTING STREAMS

◔◍◕

RANDY CLARK

R andy Clark was used of God to birth the "Toronto Blessing" in 1994. This opened the door for him to become an international speaker, who has spoken in 36 nations. From 1994-2004 Randy focused on leading renewal meetings throughout the United States and around the world where he equipped pastors and leaders of apostolic networks and denominations. He equipped them by teaching them how to pray for the sick and deliverance, receive words of knowledge, and giving them a biblical basis for healing.

However, the most important aspect of his ministry was when Randy would teach about impartation (the ability for the gifts or anointing to be transferred from one person to another person determined by the will of God) and then pray for impartation for the pastors and leaders. Since 2004 Randy has focused primarily on conducting Schools of Healing and Impartation, offering three different schools each with its own focus. Randy speaks at conferences primarily focusing on renewal, healing, and impartation.

His vision to have a training school finally came to pass when the Global School of Supernatural Ministry was founded. This school helps prepare people for work as missionaries, church planters, pastors, or in the market place with a stronger anointing for prophetic and healing ministry. This school is patterned after the School of Supernatural Ministry under Bill Johnson's oversight in Redding, California.

In 2005, Randy started the Apostolic Network of Global Awakening, a network of churches and itinerant ministries. He is the founder of Global Awakening, through which he conducts his international and national ministry.

In 2008, the School of Worship was founded to help prepare worship leaders and musicians for church planting, worship leading in churches, and itinerant worship or ministry of music opportunities.

Randy Clark shares with you the amazing power of God:

THE RIVER OF HEALING

The Bible uses the analogy of a river that has healing proper-
ties associated with it and the leaves of the trees that grow on
its banks in Ezekiel 47:12 and Revelation 22:2. This river analogy
has been used for moves of God, and as a metaphor for the
healing movement of God. I believe there is a great River of
Healing that has been released on the earth through God's
Church. However, there is a great deal of prejudice within the
Church regarding this river. And, to be honest, the flow of this
river has caused a lot of controversy and division within the
Church.

It is my desire to show how the various streams that make up
this mighty river flow into the River of Healing. One of the problems we have faced is mistaking the smaller river or creek that we are
in and feel comfortable with, for the river itself, and often seeing
other smaller rivers or creeks as foul or polluted tributaries that don't
really flow into the same River of Healing as our does.

What do I believe these valid contributing smaller rivers are
which flow into the great River of Healing within Christianity?
They are:

- healing through sacraments (Roman Catholic and
  Orthodox and others);

- healing in answer to prayers for the sick by the
  church or the elders (historical reformation
  denominations);

- healing through faith in God's promises and
  confessing and appropriating the promises by
  faith, also praying the prayer of faith for others

(Faith Cure Movement and the Word of Faith Movement);

- healing through the prayers of persons with the gifts of healing and one's own faith to receive (Pentecostalism);

- healing through the healing evangelists (Latter Rain Movement and 1948 Healing Revival);

- healing through Christians who move in the gifts of healing and/or words of knowledge (Third Wave Evangelical and Vineyard).

I believe that each of these streams is a valid stream that flows into God's great River of Healing. Are they all pure without any pollution from humankind? No, there is some of man's pollution in every one of them, but we must discern what is pollution from man, and what is the water of healing from God. We need to work to remove the pollution, clean up the rivers, and not refuse to receive the blessing they are intended to carry.

I am hoping to present the best of each river, or to legitimize each contributing river so that we can honor our other brothers and sisters in the Church Jesus died to establish, creating more unity within His Body. I believe that this greater unity will also bring about a greater flow of the River of Healing. Unity opens the windows of Heaven to the blessing of God's rain to fall and flow into all the rivers of healing. I hope to accomplish this task not so much through definitions and analysis, but through story, *my* story. You see, I have experienced or been part of almost all of these smaller rivers of healing that flow into His River of Healing. It is a humbling thing to realize that "your river" doesn't exhaust His River.

HISTORIC DENOMINATIONS—
SOFT CESSATIONISM AND LIBERALISM

My story begins in the Baptist denominations (General Baptist, Southern Baptist, and American Baptist). I always believed in healing; I can't remember a time I didn't believe in it. My maternal grandmother told me about hearing God's voice audibly telling her to go into the bedroom to pray and He would heal her. She did so and she said it felt like a hot hand went down her throat causing the large goiter to instantly disappear.

We watched Oral Roberts' healing crusades in the big tent on television, and I can remember times when the whole church would pray for someone's healing. However, I didn't understand that the churches I attended really embraced a form of what today would be called "soft cessationism." The pastors, churches, and congregations believed God could heal today. The Holy Spirit could in His sovereignty move in answer to prayer and heal the persons we prayed for as a congregation. There were no healing services, and if you had introduced them into the order of the service on any regularity you probably would have had problems with the Baptist Association or the Presbytery of the General Baptist.

The soft Cessationist belief held that the gifts of healing no longer existed in the Church, the office of healer no longer existed and tongues, prophecy, words of knowledge, working of miracles, had all ended. The interesting thing is that within the small General Baptist church that I was raised in several people moved in prophecy and/or words of knowledge, but didn't realize that they operated in these gifts. While denying the "charismatic or Pentecostal" terms for the gifts, they were actually functioning in them. They would communicate these impressions, these knowings, as "God told me," "the Lord was showing me," "I believe the Lord was leading me" type of language.

I discovered that we often expressed a reality in our hymnology that we wouldn't feel comfortable with in our theology. For example, the gospel song, "I Come to the Garden" with the lyrics, "I come to the garden alone, while the dew is still on the roses. And He talks with me and He walks with me, and He tells me I am His own." There was a belief in being led by God. The pastors of these churches I grew up in were not educated, they had no degrees from seminary, nor from college, actually most didn't have a high school education. I was 16 before the church had a pastor with a college education. Though the pastors were not educated they had been influenced by soft cessationism.

God could heal as the sovereign Lord. He might answer our prayers, "If it was His will for this person." We believed in healing enough to pray for the sick, but there wasn't a strong faith for healing. With this theology for healing we had no place for healing in the normal order of service. The pastors didn't feel any need to learn how to cooperate with the Holy Spirit or the gifts of the Spirit pertaining to healing.

There were a few times when we gathered to pray for a sick person at the front of the church in "united corporate prayer." I can think of only about 10 times in 20 years. Healing was possible, the Holy Spirit was still active in the Church, and He could heal. But, it wasn't "normative"—possible yes, normative no! Consequently we didn't see very many people healed; we didn't understand, but believed the lack of healing was connected to the will of God. He didn't seem to be very willing.

I knew God had healed my grandmother. I never forgot the story of her healing she told me when I was five years old. I believe God had also healed my Sunday school teacher when I was 12. However when I was 16 and the same people prayed for my grandfather who had cancer, he wasn't healed and died a very painful death. My theology at that time and for the next couple of years was, "God heals saintly grandmothers and Sunday school teachers who have a passionate love for him and are very spiritual, but not normal people who aren't so close to Him." Essentially my 16- to 18-year-old perspective was: God has special ones who are special to Him because they love Him in a special way, and they get special treatment like healing.

This viewpoint was shattered, though, when I was 18. I was almost killed in a car accident. I had severe skull and facial bone structure damage, multiple lacerations to the face, 10-20 percent compression of the vertebrae in my mid-spine, paralysis of my digestive system, and other injuries. I was supposed to be in the hospital for 50-80 days because of the seriousness of my injuries, but I kept telling people that I was going to attend the special evangelistic meetings at church in 28 days. Long story short—through prayers I was healed and out of the hospital in 20 days.

I went straight to church that first night out of the hospital to testify to my physical healing. The doctor had told me to go home and stay in bed. I told him he wasn't the one (I actually had a team of three specialists treating me) who healed me, God was; and I was going to go to church to praise Him and testify to my healing. (The full story of my healing is in the book, *Lighting Fires*.[1])

This experience overturned my personal view of healing. I wasn't a saintly grandmother, nor was I a Sunday school teacher, nor did I have a special relationship or commitment to God when I was healed. I had actually just experienced a rededication to God one week before the accident. I didn't deserve the healing. But, I had been healed. The healing resulted in my calling into the ministry, and within three months of the accident I was in a different college no longer pursuing a teaching degree, but in a Christian college pursuing the ministry, majoring in religious studies.

This brings me to my next crisis of faith and challenge to my views of healing. From January 1974 to December 1977 I was training for ministry majoring in religious studies in the General Baptist College and then seminary at Southern Baptist Theological Seminary. Almost all of my professors were liberal in their teaching. By liberal I mean they embraced a view that God doesn't break into our world in response to prayer in a way that would violate the

"Laws of Nature" which He had established. Not only was there little expectation of miracles today, some believed the miracles in the Bible were only legendary or mythological.

This liberalism almost destroyed my Christian faith. At one point I no longer believed in real demons, angels, or nature miracles, even those recorded in the Bible. So what was it that kept me from losing my faith? My healing—I could never doubt that God had healed me. My healing was a contradiction of the liberalism I was being influenced by in college and seminary. I was either an evangelist or pastoring throughout my theological education. I even saw God heal one of my friends while on a ministry team trip in Flint, Michigan, in a small General Baptist Church. But, again, this was definitely an exception, healing wasn't normative.

I believe that unfortunately the majority of seminary-trained ministers within the Presbyterian Church USA, most of the Southern Baptist Theological Seminaries until the early 1980s, Methodist, United Church of Christ, and many of the Lutheran Seminaries, excluding Concordia in St. Louis; and many other denominations produced several generations of ministers who have little faith for anything supernatural to happen. They do not believe in healing today and even doubt the stories of it in biblical texts.

Little wonder there is so little faith for healing in the services of the mainline denominational churches that have been influenced by liberal teaching based on the "higher-critical method" of studying the Bible. Several years after graduating seminary I wrote the following regarding the insights I had gained about the basis for this liberal way of interpreting the Bible.

There is also a quote from a term paper I wrote while in seminary that resulted in a long discussion with the professor of New Testament. He told me that I seemed very strongly committed to healing and that this subject would cause me problems in the Baptist denomination. He told me "healing is not central to the gospel; it is only peripheral." I told him I believed he was wrong, that healing was central to the gospel. He was right about one thing, however; healing did get me in trouble in the Baptist denomination.

THE HISTORICAL-CRITICAL METHOD: INTERPRETING THE BIBLE AND THE MIRACULOUS

Studying religion at college and later studying at a Baptist seminary, I was taught that the proper method of interpreting the Bible was to use the historical-critical method. This method involved studying the historical setting, studying the meaning of the original languages (Greek and Hebrew), and studying the source critics, form critics, text critics, etc.

However, one of the unspoken presuppositions of this method is its naturalistic, philosophical bias. The supernatural is not accepted because the method's presuppositions are based upon Aquinas' synthesis of Aristotelian philosophy (which had no room for the supernatural) and the Christian faith. Walter Wink states in his book, *The Bible in Human Transformation: Toward a New Paradigm for Biblical Study,* "Historical biblical criticism is bankrupt." He further states, "The historical critical method had a vested interest in undermining the Bible's authority, that it operated as a background ideology for the demystification of religious tradition, that it required functional atheism for its practice, and that its attempted mastery of the object was operationally analogous to the myth of Satan and the legend of Faust."

It was Van Harvey in his book, *The Historian and the Believer: The Morality of Historical Knowledge and Christian Belief,* who first made me aware of the logical consequence of applying the historical method completely to the biblical text. The result would be the denial of anything supernatural including the incarnation and the resurrection. Dr. Frank Tupper (my former professor at Southern Baptist Theological Seminary), in a lecture during the course on "Biblical Authority and the Modern Mind," expressed faith in the resurrection as a historical fact. However, he tended to see the miracles as mythological and legendary. It is apparent that Dr. Tupper here is following Dr. Pannenberg of South Africa.

I do not see how one can accept the resurrection and deny the miraculous. Dr. Tupper stated in his lecture, "The unusual event of the resurrection will be analogous to the experience of all in the consummation." However, healing will also be analogous to all our experiences at that time.

While writing a term paper in seminary on "The Relation of the Problem of Miracle to New Testament Interpretation and Christian Faith" for Dr. John Polhill, I made the following statement: "The incarnation is the miracle of miracles. If our world system is open so that the incarnation can occur, then it is open for miracles to occur." Dr. Polhill stated in his lectures on "The miracle stories in the Gospels," that his problem in regard to miracles deals with the incarnation. How can Jesus be fully man and have the power to perform miracles? How could modern man identify with that kind of Jesus?"

At that time I tried to resolve the problem by pointing to the dual nature of Jesus and quoting the orthodox position of the Council of Nicea A.D. 325, that Jesus was "very man of very man and very God of very God, without being a tertian quid." I now realize that the answer is that Jesus did miracles by the power of the Holy Spirit. That same power is available to all believers today. Jesus was not able to do anything of his own accord (see John 5:19,30; 8:28). Only what he saw the Father doing could He do. Before His baptism in power at the river Jordan He performed no miracles (see Luke 5:17b). He did His mighty deeds through the anointing power of the Holy Spirit. This view is based upon the Kenotic passage of Philippians 2, and is very important for our understanding of Jesus being our model for ministry. He was dependent upon the Holy Spirit. Jesus has given that same Spirit to us to enable us to fulfill the Great Commission of Matthew 28:19-20.

THE IN-BREAK OF THE KINGDOM OF GOD AND MIRACLES

If in the life and ministry of Jesus, the in-break (the Kingdom of God breaking into the kingdom of this world, which Paul alluded to as the kingdom of the devil, the god of this world) of the Kingdom of God occurred, then it seems natural that there would be conflict between Jesus and the evil forces in humankind and nature. It was because a conflict actually did occur and Jesus was victorious, that the early church attributed Lordship to Him. If these conflicts had not occurred I would be most skeptical of the idea that in Jesus the in-break of the Kingdom occurred. Without the miraculous, Jesus would be just another moral prophet like Gandhi of India, or Buddha, and nothing more to me. He would be only one of the great religious leaders of the world.

The miraculous element in Christianity and the belief that God can act in this world of ours is essential to the vitality of Christianity. Without this aspect, prayer becomes meaningless. One should study the social sciences rather than the Bible, and Theology should be replaced with Anthropology. Preaching which is void of miraculous concepts is one reason for the phenomenal growth of the Charismatic Movement, a movement reacting to the dead orthodoxy of much of Christianity. Just as Jeremiah criticized the Jews for creating with their hands gods who were helpless, modern man has created a "god" who is helpless to act in this world, a "god" whom I refuse to bow down and worship.

DEAD ORTHODOXY

Today I would change the prior paragraph that was written in 1976 from "the phenomenal growth of the Charismatic Movement" to "the phenomenal spread of the New Age Movement also caused by the dead orthodoxy of much of Christianity." A generation has arisen that is looking even more for the reality of God's presence, they can no longer be satisfied with propositional truths about God—they want to experience God.

One other insight that is strange but true is that the two opposite sides of the theological pendulum swing from liberalism to fundamentalism (which is Cessationist in its understanding of healing), ending up at the same place. Neither the pastor trained in liberalism nor the pastor trained in a fundamentalist Bible school would have healing services in their churches. They would not try to learn how to flow in the gifts of the Spirit and would not feel a need to equip the saints for the work of the ministry (at least the healing ministry) because they would not believe in it.

The liberal pastor would not attempt any of these because he believes God never violates the laws of nature. The fundamentalist pastor who believes the Bible is the inerrant word of God in all aspects of life, and who believes in the miracles and healings as historical events, would also not pursue these practices because he typically believes that gifts of healing ended with the death of the Apostles, and that miracles were given to establish the truth of the gospel and the Church and therefore don't occur in our day. Once the Scriptures were established, miracles and healing had served their purpose and weren't to be expected any longer. The liberal and the fundamentalist have become "strange bed-fellows" when it comes to healing.

I continued after graduation from seminary to pastor within the American Baptist denomination until 1984 when I was 32 years old. I ministered under the Baptist covering for 14 years. I was privileged to get to know some wonderful people, made many friends, and learned a lot about the struggles people and families go through. I have a great respect for the office of pastor. I also came to the end of myself, my abilities, my limitations, and my ministry. I had stood by many a hospital bed during those 14 years, conducted funerals for loved ones of my parishioners and parishioners themselves. I had prayed for some to be healed, but had seen little healing.

Finally I was led by the Holy Spirit to invite someone to my church I had never heard of, but whom God confirmed. I believed God had spoken to me to do three things. *One,* preach differently. No more three points and a poem, but instead teach on larger passages from the Gospels. *Two,* teach people that God still heals. *Three,* have a conference at my church on healing. These impressions were so strong that I was shaken.

YOU ARE INVITED

I wrote a letter and sent it to all the American Baptist pastors in the Midwest, and the Evangelical pastors in southern Illinois, and purposely didn't invite the Pentecostals or the Charismatics. I didn't want the Evangelical pastors to be scared off by the greater freedom of expression of the Pentecostals or Charismatics. The invitation: "If you have felt like there has to be more power for healing than what you are experiencing and are tired of going to the hospital and praying for God to guide the surgeon's hand. And, if you want to learn how to pray more effectively for physical healing, then come to this seminar."

I was surprised by the turn out at the three-day seminar. The church was filled with pastors and leaders, as well as members of my own church. God showed up and filled many. I had never seen power like this before. I personally received an impartation for words of knowledge, and for healing from the speaker, Blaine Cook, who was one of the most anointed leaders in the Vineyard Movement. I learned in those three days not only about the gift of healing that could be imparted to others, but also about the gift of impartation. Since then I have given invitations modeled after the one when I was so powerfully touched by the Holy Spirit.

Five months later I felt led of the Holy Spirit to leave the Baptist denomination and go to a city and plant a church—a call I had since I was 18. I thank God for everything that happened to mess up my comfortable nest to prepare me to step out of my comfort zone and follow Him.

THE VINEYARD MOVEMENT—
THE THIRD WAVE MOVEMENT

I joined the Vineyard Movement and became a leader in the early days of the movement. Its leader, John Wimber, was an amazing man. He loved God, honored Christ, had fellowship with the Holy Spirit and wanted to experience everything the Bible told us was possible. I had opportunities to join several Pentecostal denominations after the powerful seminar at my Baptist church, but I felt God was leading me into the Vineyard.

I liked the theology of the Vineyard regarding healing. There was a strong emphasis not to hype the meetings, never to exaggerate the claims, to learn how to move in the supernatural naturally. I felt like the Vineyard was on the cutting edge of what God was doing. It was a place to go and fit in if you were an evangelical who had been filled with the Holy Spirit, who embraced all today's gifts of the Holy Spirit, and who wanted to be involved in healing, casting out demons, ministering to the poor, and planting churches. There was also a great allowance for doctrinal diversity.

You could embrace all the gifts, the signs and wonders, healing and miracles, but you didn't have to believe that tongues was the necessary initial evidence of the Holy Spirit's baptism. (There was a strong emphasis on the value of tongues and the utility of the gift, and at one point there were more people in the Vineyard, percentage wise, speaking in tongues than in some Pentecostal denominations.) I loved it. I loved being a "Third Wave Evangelical" as we called ourselves. (Third Wave Evangelicals believe that all the gifts have continued to the present day—unlike Evangelicals who believe that what they call the "sign gifts" have ended: tongues, interpretation of tongues, prophecy, gifts of healings, and working of miracles have ended, according to these Evangelicals. They also reinterpret words of knowledge and words of wisdom so as not to have any supernatural dimension to them.)

For the first time in my life I could say that healing had become normative, it was no longer the exception, it was no longer rare. I loved this season of my life, and for 18 years continued within the Vineyard Movement. I have tried to remain true to the essential values that I saw in John Wimber and I learned in the Vineyard. I loved and continue to love the understanding of healing being in the Kingdom of God. That healing was both now and not yet. I loved the emphasis that healing was learning how to co-labor with Jesus; that we were not able to do anything in ourselves, but only what we saw the Father doing.

To this day I still don't like exaggeration of claims, hype, manipulation, pride or bragging. I still believe in everything John Wimber taught me, but I believe in more than he taught me. My pursuit of more anointing had led me out of the Baptist denomination and in 1993 would lead me to look outside the Vineyard Movement.

I heard of a man who was being used of God to bring refreshing and joy to burned-out Christians, and I certainly qualified. A friend told me about evangelist Rodney Howard-Brown from South Africa. He told me about the bizarre phenomena that occurred in his meetings, and that Rodney had said God had told him, "You will lay your hands on 1,000 pastors who will receive the anointing and will help you take revival all over the world."

I wanted to be one of the thousand. I asked my friend, "What has been the fruit of this experience in your life?" He responded, "I have seen more people healed in the past two weeks since I returned from Rodney's meetings than I have seen in the past eight years." God knew how to hook me, catch my attention, and create new hunger in my soul for Him.[2]

Within a few months the word was out that I had received a powerful impartation from Rodney, and the power of the Holy

Spirit was falling in my church. It had also fallen at the annual Regional Vineyard Pastors Conference I attended, resulting not only in people being refreshed in a very powerful manner, but also people being healed. This opened the door to go to the Airport Vineyard in Toronto for a four-day meeting. I went, God showed up, and the people began to come. The first night a woman was healed of a terminal illness. The meetings were extended until approximately ten and a half years later the meetings that had continued six nights a week came to an end. It became the longest series of protracted meetings in the history of North America.

The Vineyard Movement's theology of healing had placed a high value on training its people for the ministry of deliverance, and healing—emotional, physical, and spiritual. The Airport Vineyard (now Airport Christian Fellowship and referred to as TACF) had one of the best-trained teams for ministry that I ever met in the Vineyard. With this new impartation and anointing I was seeing more healings than I had in several years.

I loved the fact that the Vineyard wasn't a one-man show, but that the ministry was dependent on trained laypersons, the saints who had been equipped for the work of ministry (see Eph. 4:11-12). This view of healing in the Vineyard required the pastors to press in for more anointing for healing, more understanding of healing, and more ability to move in the gifts that often were associated with healing, especially words of knowledge. It also had an affect upon the order of service, the liturgy of the church.

Usually after a time of worship in the congregational meeting or a small home meeting there would be a pause to see if someone had received a word of knowledge regarding a physical healing, or a prophetic word that might help someone receive an emotional healing. Often the ministry team would be invited to the front of the church before the invitation, and the invitation was often very broad including inviting people to come for healing prayer as well as to repent for their sins.

It was believed that healing was not in the cross like forgiveness of sins was, but it was *through* the cross, through Jesus' passion that healing was made available. Healing was seen to be the will of God because Jesus had taught us to pray the Lord's Prayer which was seen to be a warfare prayer, "...Thy Kingdom come, Thy will be done, on earth as it is in heaven." Though it was admitted that sometimes God could let us know that the sickness someone had was unto death, this was more the exception, and was not thought to be normative.

Healing was to be expected as part of the proclamation of the good news of the in-break of the Kingdom of God in the earth. It was not enough for a pastor to teach or preach about the Kingdom. The Vineyard pastor needed and desired to be able to demonstrate the power of the Kingdom of God. This was no safe place for the timid of heart. As Wimber would so often say, "Faith is spelled: R-I-S-K."

I remained in the Vineyard from 1984 to 2001—18 growing, productive, challenging, and maturing years.

THE WORD OF FAITH MOVEMENT

In October 1994 in Berry, Ontario, my wife, DeAnne, and I were at a meeting with John and Carol Arnott, Wes and Stacey Campbell, and Mark Dupont. We had all gone to a hotel room to pray and fellowship. During this time Mark Dupont gave me a prophetic word that soon came to pass. It had come to him in a vision. The word was encouraging and part of it was, "Your ministry is about to change. You are about to begin ministering with the Pentecostals, Assemblies, and Word of Faith. And, I know your testimony, I know that last one will be hard for you to accept, but in the near future God is going to open to you a door to the Pentecostals, Assemblies, and the Word of Faith."

I responded, "If that happens that will have to be God. I don't know any Pentecostals, my theology isn't classical Pentecostal, and

I don't even like the Word of Faith Movement. It would be a miracle if that happened." Up until that time all my invitations were coming from the Vineyard, after this prophecy it immediately went from 100 percent Vineyard to 10 percent Vineyard invitations. The invitations were now coming from Pentecostals, Charismatics, Word of Faith, and some large Baptist, Lutheran, Roman Catholic, and Independents, but the majority were from the Pentecostals and Assemblies.

God was teaching me things. I had gone to the leaders of the Rhema Church in Tulsa, Oklahoma, where I had gone to hear Rodney Howard-Brown, to ask them to forgive me for all the mean-spirited things I had said about the Word of Faith Movement, and to tell them that I wouldn't speak badly about them anymore. God had dealt with me about my spirit, but I still thought my theology was right and Word of Faith wasn't correct or at least was unhealthy. My problem was my experience had been negative in regard to the Word of Faith message. Now God was going to let me see the positive side of Word of Faith. God would arrange it so that I would end up listening to someone tell about how they had received a significant healing, from confessing the promises of God. For a while it seemed like everywhere I went I kept meeting Word of Faith people who had been healed of terminal illness through standing in faith. I took note of these coincidences, while not really believing in coincidences.

Sometime around 1999 I began to question my position on healing that I had been so comfortable with in the Vineyard. I began to see that the "Kingdom Now but Not Yet" teaching was actually lowering people's expectation for healing. I also began to realize that there had been other more powerful movements and personalities that had seen more healings than John Wimber. And almost all of them believed healing was both in the cross of Jesus as well as His Kingdom. Kingdom now but not yet, was in actuality only a step away from believing that healing is determined by the sovereignty of God.

I became convinced that He was much more willing to heal than our experiences demonstrated. I also thought that the Vineyard and Third Wave Evangelicals were too easily convinced that God wasn't doing anything if they (we) didn't see it immediately when we prayed for the person. We had learned how to recognize the effects of the Holy Spirit upon the body. If we didn't see those phenomena we often assumed God wasn't doing anything in this person.

I met Joe McIntyre in 2003. Joe is an apostolic leader in the Word of Faith Movement. Bill Johnson gave me Joe's book, *E.W. Kenyon and His Message of Faith, the True Story*, to read. I read it all, including every footnote. Many false understandings I had about Word of Faith teaching were corrected. I gained a true historical understanding of the origins of the confession-possession teaching. I discovered it wasn't rooted in new thought, unity, or Christian Science, but rather was rooted in the best teaching among evangelicals in the latter half of the 19th century; men like D.L. Moody, R.A. Torrey, A.J. Gordon, A.B. Simpson, George Mueller, and others.

The teaching was actually rooted in the 19th century Holiness Movement and the shorter way to sanctification as taught by Mrs. Phoebe Palmer. Her teaching was that the way to enter into sanctification was to receive it by faith, confess it as true until it manifested in your life. She understood that the way we receive justification is the same way we receive sanctification, by faith apart from feelings, and with the confession with our lips to the reality. Both are benefits to us through the cross of Jesus. It was only one more step to move from justification and sanctification to believing that this is the same way we receive healing.

Trusting and believing in the covenant promises of God provided in the cross of Jesus, and confessing those promises as already received, while waiting patiently for the manifestation of faith's confession was how to receive healing. It wasn't sensory denial, but confessing a greater truth than what the sick person was experiencing physically. It wasn't denying truth, merely believing in a greater truth.

Long phone discussions and later personal discussions with Joe helped me to see my real issue wasn't with the Word of Faith message, but the poor pastoral applications of this message causing people to feel bad about their faith and themselves if they weren't healed, and the overemphasis upon prosperity that was becoming all too common.

I soon discovered that I had spoken the wrong words from my pulpit about the Word of Faith Movement. I had formed the wrong impressions about the movement from my limited experience and I had received wrong information from faulty historical sources that purported to be scholarly.

The Word of Faith message would impact the liturgy or order of the service and pastors in the following ways: the pastor would be strong on teaching the word in order to build confidence in God, His promises, His provision, and His plan for healing. The Word of Faith Movement, like the Faith Cure Movement, would not so much emphasize the healing evangelist with his anointing, or the gifts of healing and words of knowledge, or even training up laypeople to pray for the sick as much as other groups would, like the Pentecostals and the Vineyard. The order of the service would have a time to come forward for healing through the prayer of faith, often prayed by the elders. But, the main emphasis was the personal responsibility for individuals to receive directly from God through personal faith.

The value of the message in the Word of Faith Movement is that it provides hope, and builds confidence or faith to receive a healing by rooting it in relationship—not mechanical confessions, but trusting relationship in God as Father. It provides a strong basis upon which to believe God for the needed healing—promises in the Word of God and the covenant of God. If you had not been healed in a prayer line by the anointed healing evangelist, had not been healed through a word of knowledge, or through team ministry; there still remained the hope and possibility of receiving healing through your own personal faith and trust in God.

There are many people who need this hope. I now understand that our opposition to this message is often an overreaction to poor pastoral applications. I realized that the promises were offered by Jesus not the latest faith teacher. I came to understand that it is better to have hope than despair, because in despair the basis of hope has been destroyed.

I believe that there is truth in the Word of Faith message, that it is one of the golf clubs we need in our bag to be more successful in our game of golf (a Wimber analogy between golf and the healing ministry). There will be times to pull this club out and use it. For this reason I often have Pastor Joe McIntyre teach the most balanced presentation on healing from the Faith Camp perspective in my Schools of Healing and Impartation. I want to bring balance to the "Now but not yet" theology of healing that is rooted in the position that healing is in the Kingdom of God which is both now, but not yet, that is, not yet fully consummated.

During the past two years I have been spending a lot of time reading about discoveries that are being made in the medical community regarding healing and spirituality. A professor of medicine at Harvard Medical School, Dr. Benson sees importance in positive confession. He uses the term "cognitive restructuring" in a very special way but meaning something very similar to the preacher in the "Word of Faith Camp." Dr. Benson is aware of the possibility for "positive restructuring" to be misunderstood and may cause some to feel as if they are responsible for not being healed by not being able to "positively restructure" their thought life. He signals a warning to keep the focus off of self and not feel guilty if healing doesn't occur. Yet, Dr. Benson believes the benefits of "positive restructuring" for people who are sick outweigh the potential for some to be hurt by the practice.[3] One can choose to judge any of these streams by their worst representatives or their best representatives, and one can decide to illustrate the lack of balance by stories that are nightmarish, boarding on the ludicrous, even embarrassing to other leaders in the Word of Faith Movement. On the other hand I can illustrate the balance within the movement with wonderful stories of the dead being raised, terminally ill being healed, and providing confidence in one's ability to accomplish great things for God.

Others have attempted to judge a movement by its roots rather than its fruit, choosing not to follow Jesus' advice for discernment. This attempt has mistakenly, due to poor historical research, claimed that the roots of the Word of Faith Movement are in New Thought, Theosophy, Christian Science, because of E.W. Kenyon's supposed connection with these groups. As I have already stated, the roots of Kenyon are in the teachings of the greatest Evangelical teachers of the last half of the 19th century, rather than the New Thought cults (McIntyre, 1997).

About the same time that I was being exposed to the Word of Faith Movement, I was also meeting and working with classical Pentecostals. God was opening the door for me to minister among the Assemblies of God, the Church of God—Cleveland, the Pentecostal Holiness, the Four Square, and the Open Bible denominations.

PENTECOSTALISM AND HEALING

Historically speaking I believe no movement has had a greater contribution to the great River of Healing as has the Pentecostal Movement. When it began it embraced the best of the teaching of the Faith Cure Movement. But it was different in that it saw itself as the fulfillment of the hope that had been expressed within Protestantism for almost a century—that right before the end of time and the coming of Jesus He would once again pour out upon His Church a great empowering anointing.

That anointing would restore not only of the gifts of the Holy Spirit, but the Ephesians 4 offices of the apostle, prophet, evangelist, pastor, and teacher. The "Latter Rain" of the Holy Spirit would be poured out. The Church had been looking forward to a new Pentecost, to a recovery of apostolic Christianity. This would be a restoration of apostolic Christianity that preceded the second coming of Jesus. This would include both "situational" and "constituted" gifts for the people of God.

It is a sad chapter that there was a negative aspect of healing during this time related to medicine and doctors. This viewpoint was also influenced by some of the teachers within the Faith Cure Movement who held to this same view. This would in time cause the majority of the populace of America to see the Pentecostal view of healing as "fanatical."

Out of this movement came the 1947 Latter Rain Movement—which strongly emphasized the equipping of the saints for ministry, training within the local church for moving in the gifts of the Holy Spirit, and an even greater emphasis upon God pouring out the Latter Rain, including the office gifts of the apostle and prophet. Some of these leaders would be used of God to break open entire nations to the gospel, like Argentina and Kenya, as well as other nations through great healings crusades and resurrections from the dead.

Out of Pentecostalism would be birthed some of the greatest healing evangelists during the 1948 Healing Revival. It is true that the impetus for this great revival came through a Baptist, William Branham, but the majority of those who saw what God was doing in Branham, who became hungry to be used like him were not Baptists, but Pentecostals.

Out of these latter two movements with their Pentecostal roots would grow a major missionary movement and church planting movement. Though the Evangelical arm of the Church thought for years this was a polluted river, time has proven and vindicated the Pentecostal's belief in a renewed Christianity.

The theology of the Pentecostal included the best of the Faith Cure Movement, which was an Evangelical movement, not a Pentecostal movement. But it also blended, as I have said, both the "situational" and "constituted" viewpoint of the gifts of the Holy Spirit. Since the Baptism of the Holy Spirit was for power to witness, it should not surprise us to learn that it produced the greatest missionary expansion in the history of Protestantism. Today about 80 percent or more of all Christians in Latin America, Africa, and Asia have Pentecostal experiences. It has been said that 80 percent of the people of Africa visited a church for the first time in order to be healed.[4] Concerned Roman Catholics noting the phenomenal growth of Pentecostals report 85 percent of the Protestant Christians are Pentecostal or Charismatic in China.[5] In Brazil, 90 percent of the non-Catholic growth of Christianity is Pentecostal.[6]

Over time the emphasis became stronger to look past the healing evangelist for healing, and look inward for healing through personal faith. It was always important to have faith. It was believed that without faith, one couldn't be healed; not even by a healing evangelist. But during this time the expectancy of being healed through one's own faith was no longer the main emphasis as it had been in the Faith Cure Movement.

About ten years after the outpouring of the Spirit in Toronto in 1994, I began to sense a calling of God to impact America's institutions of higher learning: universities, seminaries, and divinity schools. I began to ask God to open the doors, and soon they did. It first began by just teaching occasionally in a university divinity school. Then the door opened to sponsor a Symposium on Healing: Catholic, Protestant, and Medical Perspectives. This was held at the University of St. Louis, the oldest university west of the Mississippi, and a Catholic university. Some professors from the medical school and the divinity school participated in the symposium as well as a research scientist from Washington University in

St. Louis. Dr. Francis and another person were invited to teach from the Catholic perspective, and I from the Protestant.

This experience powerfully impacted me. I wanted to have more opportunities to speak to clergy, the medical professionals, and students of both the medical and the divinity schools. I began to study more about what modern medical science was discovering about healing, and how this information aligned with the biblical understanding of healing. I also learned that there was a strong New Age type of emphasis on healing occurring in colleges and universities.

God is opening the door for ministry in colleges and universities. I have received inquires and invitations from professors or head chaplains of six universities in the last three years. In addition to the symposium on Healing: Spiritual and Medical Perspectives, I also began conducting Schools of Healing and Impartation with three different schools, each with their own unique emphasis. This opened the door to learning more about Roman Catholicism and the Orthodox church.

ROMAN CATHOLIC AND ORTHODOX

In 2005 while preparing to teach the material for the Schools of Healing and Impartation, I became much more aware of the role healing played in the Catholic church before its split into the Roman Catholic and Orthodox branches. The major three ways healing has occurred in this part of the Church of Jesus Christ have been through the sacraments, especially the sacrament of the Eucharist (Lord's Supper), the sacrament of Healing (based upon James 5), and healing in connection to reliquaries (the honored place which holds the bones of saints). Actually, in the Middle Ages the majority of healings seemed to be connected to prayers offered at the reliquary.

Anytime someone is healed in Jesus' name or with an understanding that healing comes from His death at the cross, I think it is a good thing. We should be slow to make judgments against Roman Catholics for this practice when we have famous Protestant evangelists who have asked us to reach out and touch the television screen to receive our healing. Whether the point of contact for the release of faith is a reliquary or the television, the principle is the same; healing is rooted in faith.

The Catholic church and the Orthodox sometimes have special services for healing, and they still have someone in the diocese to perform deliverances. Since Vatican II the sacrament of Last Rites has been restored to the Sacrament of Healing.

There is little emphasis on the priest to equip the parishioners about how to pray for each other. There is little expectation that the local priest be anointed to heal the sick or understand how to move in the gifts of the Holy Spirit. Even so, there are many priests in the Roman Catholic Church who are Spirit filled and move in the gifts of the Holy Spirit. However, the liturgy of the Roman Catholic Church for the Mass does not allow time or place for such gifts to operate. The gifts would be relegated to special meetings or prayer groups in the parish.

When I first led a team on a healing trip it was to assist John Wimber. I remember he told us that the Roman Catholics were the easiest to receive healing because their Church had never believed healings had stopped. I have found that Roman Catholics do receive healing more easily than some Protestants.

CONCLUSION

Liberal denominations and pastors do not expect God to heal because of an anti-supernatural bias. They see prayer as not affecting God, but affecting us. The prayer of the pastor is for the comfort of the sick person, aimed for his ear rather than the ear of God. There is little expectation in the hearts of the parishioners who have sat under the teaching and preaching of such pastors. The church services (liturgy) do not have healing services included, nor are there special services for prayer. This is generally true, but some pastors are so liberal as to embrace healing from non-Christian sources like Reiki and/or therapeutic touch. They are open to New Age and quasi-scientific approaches to healing. This position can be likened to a polluted stream running into the River of Healing.

The strongest version of cessationism has the least to commend it (excluding liberalism) because it does the most harm to the hope for healing of the parishioner and priest or pastor. This view of healing is likened to a small stream with barely any water in it leading into the great River of Healing. There is almost no expectation of healing, and no expectation of someone having the gift, anointing, or power to heal. There is no theological basis to expect a healing; instead there is a theological basis *not* to expect healing.

This view, which is held among the Reformation denominations as well as the Restoration Movement—Church of Christ, Disciples of Christ, and Christian Church—is being modified. There is growing pressure to move away from a strong Cessationist position to a soft Cessationist position where there is recognition that the Holy Spirit is still alive, and can answer prayers for healing according to the will of God. There is a growing understanding that healing is part of the expression of the message of the Kingdom.

Still there is a rejection of gifts of healing in the church today and of persons with the gift of healing or the ability to work miracles. While rejecting the possibility of a person moving in these gifts, they believe God can still work miracles and healings in answer to prayer. Some who hold to this view even make room in the services for a time when the elders lay hands on the sick after anointing with oil and pray for healing. The elders aren't seen as having the gift of healing, but as following the James 5 biblical admonition to do so as elders.

The people who hold to this modified position of cessationism have more hope, faith, and expectancy that God might heal in answer to prayer. This position is like a Midwest creek that is quite small but running with a little water into the River. There is more expectation of healing happening in response to prayer because the teaching from the pulpit has more emphasis on the role of the Holy Spirit as continuing the works of Jesus on the earth in response to faith and the prayers of the saints.

Unlike the harder Cessationist viewpoint which restricts or sees the Holy Spirit's role today as only in relationship to salvation, this softer Cessationist viewpoint sees the Holy Spirit having more to do today than simply His relationship to salvation with all its dimensions: convicting of sin, righteousness, and judgment; calling or awakening the sinner; regeneration; sealing, baptizing into the Body of Christ, filling, sustaining, and guiding. This view sees the Holy Spirit still carrying out the will of God the Father and the Son on the earth. He still could heal, deliver, and in the place where the gospel was being heard for the first time, even work miracles.

The Third Wave Movement, of which the Vineyard would be a major expression, is a new source of water, an underground spring that suddenly burst forth providing fresh water to a Northeastern large creek, (which are as large as small rivers in the Midwest). For awhile there was a great amount of water flowing in this tributary to the River of Healing. The pastors and the people rejected Cessationism, and believed in healing, in gifts of healing, in impartations for a stronger anointing for healing, and in authority for deliverance. There was a lot of teaching about healing, training for ministry of the laity—the emphasis was upon "equipping the saints for the work of ministry." As John Wimber said, "Everybody gets to play." "We all get to do the stuff."

The emphasis was upon the Holy Spirit's ability to give the person a gift of healing for the situation. The view was referred to as "situational gifting" like a plumber who goes to do a job and whatever tool is needed at the job would be provided in that situation, but the plumber didn't get to carry the tool chest. The plumber was dependent upon the Holy Spirit to provide the needed tool/gift. The movement is uncomfortable with the idea of constituted gifts— the plumber always has the tools with him. The emphasis is not on the healing evangelist but on the "healing by the laity."

This movement has a solid, biblical theology of healing being in the Kingdom, being both "now but not yet." This means that healing is available because it is in the Kingdom, but the Kingdom hasn't yet been consummated, it hasn't come in its fullness—that time when all sickness and disease will be done away with, when we will all be changed, and given glorified bodies. Only then will we all be healed. Until the consummation, the healings we see are "signs" of what is to happen in the consummation when Jesus returns.

Tragically, this tributary doesn't flow with the volume of water that it originally did when it began. There seems to have been a retreat on the part of the pastors from the initial emphasis upon healing, the gifts, and the powerful impartations. The parishioners in this movement were once expectant for the supernatural, but the expectancy has waned.

The pastors in the Third Wave Movement are not as expectant as they once were of moving in the gifts of the Holy Spirit. In the words of one executive pastor of a large church in the Third Wave stream, "the people are caught in a vicious cycle. Their theology hasn't changed, they still biblically believe in signs and wonders, healings and the manifestations of the Holy Spirit, but they don't have the same living expectation for them to occur today as they did several years ago. They are caught in a vicious cycle. With each passing year their experience is less than their biblical theology of healing, and with each passing year their experience becomes less, due to their expectation. And, with the expectation dropping lower the following year they see even less miracles and healings, which in turn causes their experience to be even lower."

When asked what I did to reverse this vicious cycle I told this executive pastor and his senior pastor that they need to get somewhere where there is a more "open heaven" for healing like certain places in Africa or South America. (At that time there wasn't as much hunger or healing in the United States as we are seeing today.)

It is my desire to see this once powerful tributary that flowed like a small river flow once again with the force it had originally—actually with even greater force.

SMALL BUT MIGHTY STREAMS

The Word of Faith Movement with its roots in the Faith Cure Movement is a valid "small River of Healing" that flows into the great River of Healing. Here there is an emphasis upon teaching the parishioners about their authority and covenantal rights through Jesus. With a strong emphasis upon teaching and understanding our covenant benefits, which include healing, the emphasis is more on the person who is sick appropriating their healing through their faith than on receiving healing through the ministry of someone else who flows in the gifts of the Holy Spirit. That includes those with gifts of healing (situational gifts), or someone who has a healing anointing who God uses for healing (constituted gifting); instead the emphasis is more upon the sick person and his/her personal faith.

Some have seen this stream or small river, as totally or mostly polluted, but I believe this view is incorrect. That isn't to say that some of the people in the movement haven't thrown some trash into the water. (Many movements have thrown trash into their tributary, not intentionally polluting their stream, but trash nonetheless.) To be fair, this movement has been one of the major "rivers" that flows into the great River of Healing. There is much more expectation for healing in this movement than in some others. It is a last bastion of hope that healing can come to those who have not been healed in other streams. The theology for healing in this stream is one of the strongest. Healing is a covenantal promise from God. Healing is available to the believer as forgiveness of sins, and both come to us by faith because of the death of Jesus. Healing is in the Cross not through it. It is believed that healing is the will of God, because Jesus healed all who came to him, and He came to reveal the Father.

The greatest tributary to the great River of Healing within Christianity is the Pentecostal river. It has a strong view of healing being in the atonement of Jesus; healing gifts are both situational and constituted, with some people even called as healing evangelists. The emphasis on healing has been a major tool of evangelism, especially in the southern hemisphere where Christianity is the strongest today and the fastest growing.

Like the Third Wave Movement, the Pentecostal Movement in the United States has also lost much, if not most, of its original emphasis on healing. I have had the opportunity to minister in many Pentecostal churches around the world. It is my opinion that many Pentecostal churches have few Pentecostal experiences anymore and have become lukewarm, having lost the "fire of Pentecost." Many of the Pentecostal churches have become seeker sensitive churches rather than healing churches.

The philosophy of ministry of the seeker-sensitive model allows little room for the working of the Holy Spirit, for healing as part of the service, or special services for healing. There is little room for the Holy Spirit to take over the service, for the order to be surrendered to His order, for the worship to just continue for the whole service, during which sovereign healings occur. The people are no longer being trained in how to pray for the sick or cast out demons.

PRAYERS

Fortunately, this is not the case for the Pentecostals of the southern hemisphere. And, I am sure there are still many on-fire Pentecostal churches in the United States, but I am concerned about the growing number that are losing the fire. I pray and hope for the River of Healing that flows out of the Pentecostal Movement to burst forth again; whatever has been at work to hinder the flow of this tributary to be removed; and for the Pentecostal tributary to once again be one of the greatest in its flow into the Great River of Healing within Christianity.

I also pray for our brothers and sisters in the Roman Catholic and Orthodox churches to experience in the present the grace of healing that has historically flowed in those churches. I want to see the Spirit fall in the great cathedrals of the world. I know two young men, Europeans—one Swiss the other French—of Pentecostal experience. They were invited by the hierarchy of the Roman Catholic church to go to Paris and minister. The Catholic leaders said, "We have something you need, and you have something we need. We have large cathedrals in Paris that are almost empty, and you have an anointing for healing." The cathedrals where they minister are filled to overflowing—and the majority of the people attending were not yet Christians.

Much of Europe has slipped into a post-Christian experience. The percentage of British population that regularly attends Christian church services is about 3 percent[7], as more and more of the population becomes either Muslim or New Age. May God wake up His Church to experience the gospel of the Kingdom of God with accompanying signs and wonders.

May we Christians find what we have in common, stop dividing over small doctrinal issues, and join together as we join our God in this greatest of all Harvest Fields. May we all learn about our authority, our position in Christ. May we experience the power of His Holy Spirit, flow in the gifts of the Holy Spirit; and may we work together across denominational lines to evangelize those who don't know about Him, don't believe He was God, don't believe He was raised from the dead, don't believe we can be forgiven because of His death.

And, may we preach and live this gospel of the Kingdom with a living expectation of signs and wonders following our lives; may we pray for this to happen among the whole Church of Jesus Christ.

ENDNOTES

1. *Lighting Fires* can be purchased online at www .globalawakening.com.

2. Ibid.

3. Herbert Benson, *Timeless Healing: The Power and Biology of Belief* (New York: Simon and Shuster Publishers, 1996), pp. 272-275.

4. Harvey Cox, *Fire From Heaven: The Rise of Pentecostal Spirituality and the Reshaping of Religion in the Twenty-First Century,* p. 247.

5. Ralph Martin, *The Catholic Church at the End of an Age: What the Spirit Is Saying,* p. 53.

6. Cox, *Fire From Heaven,* p. 168.

7. Dale Hurd, "Is Europe the New Dark Continent?" http:// www.cbn.com/CBNNews/News/040301a.aspx; accessed 9/25/08.

Chapter 3

THE POWER OF HIS PRESENCE

⊂◈⊃

CAROL AND CHRISTY WIMBER

Carol and John Wimber were married 42 years before his passing in 1997. Carol and John worked together in much of the birth and growth of the Vineyard Movement. Carol is the author of *The Way It Was*, the story behind the man, and how the Vineyard came about.

Christy Wimber, Carol's daughter-in-law, has been involved with the Vineyard Movement since the beginning. She worked for years at Vineyard Ministries and Vineyard Music. She and her husband, Sean, oversee Doin' the Stuff (DTS), which handles John Wimber materials as well as others in the Vineyard Movement. Christy and Carol released a DVD,

"Back to our Roots," which covers the history of the Vineyard Movement. She also just released a book with John Wimber's teachings, *The Way In Is the Way On*. She teaches at conferences and retreats worldwide.

CAROL'S STORY

When looking back at what made the Vineyard distinctive, I realize it was primarily our understanding of the Christian life. In the Quaker church in which John and I were saved, there was no higher call than to be a Christian. The man who led us to the Lord used to talk about the responsibility and the wonder that we walked around with—the presence of God dwelling in us.

Also in that Quaker church there was simplicity, and a lack of ambition. The man who led us to the Lord was a welder. The foundation of the church was everyday, simple people. They dressed down; they drove Chevys instead of Cadillacs, even though some of them were quite wealthy. Everyone felt comfortable and welcome. There was no great gap between the clergy and the laity. We didn't even use those words in the Quaker church. The focus was whether we would love people, how we led our lives before them, and whether our faith was real.

The truth is the Holy Spirit really began to visit us in the Quaker church. It sometimes sounds or comes across as if nothing was happening before this time, but that wasn't the case. There had been an increased hunger in us for God and for His Word. But there was also a huge increase of hunger to worship. In the Quaker worship, they have what they call "communion." This is a time of silence when they wait and soak in God, unless someone has a song from the Lord, or a word, or even a teaching.

When someone receives something, they would speak it out. Every once in awhile someone would sing out a beautiful song or have a short teaching or some sort of revelation—though they don't call it that.

So we were no strangers to the move of the Spirit—in fact the later outpouring was merely an increase of what had already been happening.

I believe the Vineyard foundation was formed on Quakerism. Most people don't realize that; in fact they believe the Vineyard came from Calvary, when in fact, we're Quakers.

When we look back and see God's presence moving on and forming us, worship played an intricate part. Over the years we've seen things change-shift, but from the very beginning we understood that worship wasn't "for" anything, except the Lord. Sometimes I get the feeling that we've shifted a bit too—we worship in order for *this* to happen. Whatever *this* is—a great move of the Spirit perhaps. But, truthfully, this is the opposite of what we were doing in the early days. We were worshiping simply because God is worthy of worship. The wonderful things that happened were as a result of His presence—we didn't worship so that His presence would come; we just worshiped!

We didn't even really know about trying to *make* things happen. That wasn't why we were meeting together. We were meeting out of love for God. It was odd to us that during the time John was teaching a course at Fuller Theological Seminary for seasoned missionaries (MC 510: Signs, Wonders, and Church Growth) that the course would become world famous and we would become "great healers." That sure wasn't anything we were doing—that's just something God did when He showed up.

Through God showing up we got this reputation, so many churches became or wanted to become Vineyards around that time, and that's what their idea of the Vineyard was. But John and I did not set out to become famous healers. John used to say, "I do what I do. I preach the gospel. I lay hands on the sick. Either God will heal them or He won't. I just do what I do, and God does what He does. Shame on me if I don't do what I do, but He's responsible for what He does or doesn't do. We're just following directions."

John had this ability to see what was coming in the days ahead, so he would often prepare or warn us what would be coming next. Concerning the Vineyard, John used to always say that an outpouring has about a 20-year life span. Then hinges will get too much in cement and we'll start building monuments to ourselves. He said, "I don't expect us to be any different. But the Lord is faithful, and He'll pour out His Spirit again and again. It may not be here, but let's all be watching and listening, and as soon as that happens, let's go where He is!"

John had great respect and regard for the whole Church and believed that the Lord's hands were on it. He knew it was possible for a movement to be sustained for hundreds of years. Look at the Moravians. But he didn't have any huge concern that we had to protect the movement. He knew that our grandchildren would find where the Lord was pouring Himself out if the presence of Jesus wasn't here anymore.

CHRISTY'S TURN

John Wimber had this great beatitude where he would say, "Blessed are the flexible." We hardly hear or use the word *flexible* anymore. In the Vineyard, we say all the time, "We only do what we see the Father doing." However, it's not about just seeing what the Father is doing, it's about *doing* what the Father is doing. If you want to see God "stuff" happen, it's not just recognizing what He's doing, or moving on, but it's also in the doing.

Romans 12:16 says this: *"but readily adjust yourself to [people, things] and give yourself to humble tasks. Never overestimate yourself or be wise in your conceits"* (AMP). The word translated as *adjust* actually means "to conform." So we are called to adapt; we're called to conform to what God is showing us. We're called to accommodate what He's speaking to us. Conform. He doesn't conform to, "Hey, Lord, I have this really great idea, and I need You to get on board here." *We* are the ones who are called to adapt and to accommodate what the Lord is speaking to us. I know how it feels coming up with a really good idea, or seeing something somewhere else that seems to be working. "Lord, see this? This worked for a lot of people, and we're starting to see some fruit from it." Perhaps the Lord is saying to do otherwise, "That has worked before, but that's not what I want you to do now!"

It's a trust issue isn't it? The truth is, if the Father shows us things and we don't do them, our clarity of hearing and seeing Him clearly begins to fade. If you want to see, you have to be faithful with what He's already shown you. Remember the Kingdom principle? Be faithful with a little, and you get more. It's difficult, in fact nearly impossible, to move in God's presence if you're not walking in obedience, sin separates us. We are called to carry His glory, His presence. Obedience is important to be a carrier.

Didn't Jesus say, "Blessed is the one who has eyes to see, and ears to hear?" Didn't He also say that we should come to Him like little children? Seems the older we get, the easier it is to get caught up in how we know things work. We get comfortable, and have little energy or passion for taking risks.

God's presence is something that comes the way He wants it to. We can either choose to be comfortable, or become a catalyst for how He chooses to move. The bottom line is the Kingdom is going to come, and we're either going to recognize it, or not. The only way that we're going to recognize when God moves is if we have eyes to see and ears to hear. Blessed are the flexible.

How things worked in the past may not be how God wants to move now. It's important to function out of His presence, rather than knowledge. Avoid getting stuck in, "This is the way we've always done it." His new way can be the road to our freedom. In the Vineyard we are called to be Kingdom people, recognizing His Spirit and adapting to that. That is the defining difference between what we call the Vineyard and so many other wonderful places of worship. Follow His Spirit in doing Kingdom stuff.

This was one of the greatest legacies John Wimber left to us! He wasn't afraid of God moving, as long as he knew it was the Lord. Even when what He was doing was different. John often "took the heat" for what God was leading him to do. Along the way, he carefully discerned what the Vineyard was to be part of, and what we weren't called to do. John wasn't afraid to go for it, or admit that he was wrong. When he was wrong, he would say it. In fact in front of everyone! I loved that about him. It stopped a lot of guessing and rumors!

Every time God has moved on us, it's been different. Just look at church history! He is different every time, and when we try to put Him in a formula and try to sell it, He changes the package. God cannot be conformed to a manmade formula.

When God moves in ways that we're not used to, it often offends us. And it brings stuff up in us that is ugly. If we're going to see what it is that He wants to do, we're going to have to lay down how we think it's supposed to look and adapt to Him. Most likely it won't be easy, and it will challenge what we feel is comfortable. The church seems to be less flexible, and the world doesn't have a hard time adjusting to new ways.

TAKE THE BEST AND GO!

John knew that we would again be in a place where we would need to know the importance of taking the best and going forward. I want to take the best that has been put in me, that's been spoken into me, and leave the rest. I don't want to live in what was. I want to be right in the middle of what God's going to do next. Don't you?

A few years ago I saw a picture from the Lord. I saw a beautiful head of nice and polished hair. Then I saw big hands come down and mess up the hairdo. I just started laughing because I thought about how that is exactly the way that it works. I felt like the Lord was saying that He is coming to mess up what we thought was so perfect (in the church). We have everything all in place, so presentable, and these big hands will come down from Heaven and mess it all up!

I see that picture every once in awhile, especially when I think, "Look, Lord, this looks good, and this sounds good." But I don't want to do things just because it's working or looks so perfect. There's some sense in that, but there's more: recognizing what the Father is doing and then doing it. Conforming to His ways.

I honestly believe that living out of His presence means that we become so connected to the Father that it would be scarier *not* to follow Him.

UNCOMPLICATE SIMPLICITY

In church, I want one of our highest values to be being purposeful in being simple, and how to stay simple. But the truth is, you can talk too much about how to be simple and make simple complicated. The gospel message is a simple message, and isn't the message power in itself? It is impossible to be flexible and follow what the Holy Spirit is showing you if everything that you're doing is very complicated.

Adjusting to God's new ways takes time and room, or it causes fear. So being able to stay simple, as easy as it sounds, is actually hard.

When the Vineyard started we didn't even have a place to meet. Every week we would meet in a different place and the people still found us. I believe that because we were willing to be part of what the Father was doing, and adjusting to Him, we could have met in a bathroom and people would have found us.

At the end of the day, people need to experience God. Programs are good, structure is not bad, but what people need is an encounter with the Living God. One of the things that Carol says to me often is, "do everything that you can in the simplest way that you can, in the cheapest way that you can." We were laughing at one point because when our church in Yorba Linda started, I said to my husband, Sean, "Let's just use John's [our son] Fisher Price microphone."

I have full confidence that if I obey what the Holy Spirit is showing me to do, everything will be all right. I mean, if the pastor doesn't believe that, then the people won't either. I completely believe that God's move doesn't have anything to do with how comfortable our chairs are, how great the air conditioning is, or what great programs we have. I'm confident that if we create an environment for the Holy Spirit to move how He desires, the people will come. I'm sold on it. You know why I'm sold on it? Because I've seen it happen time and time again.

I've also seen the other side. We've worked really hard before to get good stuff going, but I hated it. I didn't understand why I hated it. It was good, the people were nice, comfy chairs, good coffee, clean building, but there was something missing. I think it was the element of risk. You and I are called to a ministry of high risk. To me risk is a gift. I can't think of a time when I got something that I believed was from the Lord, and somebody didn't say to me, "Christy, you are crazy; that will never work; what the heck are you thinking?"

At the end of the day it comes down to whether or not I will do what I'm seeing or not. One of the many things that happens when the Holy Spirit comes on me is that I break out in a red rash. Not a lot of glory in that. I don't know why it happens but I know it's from the Lord. My prayer is, "Lord, don't let me stop this if it's You."

WISDOM IN WAITING

I think it's important to remember that building anything apart from the Holy Spirit will most likely end up draining you. The Vineyard didn't start because John and Carol wanted a movement. It was initiated by the Holy Spirit.

Whatever you build yourself, you will have to maintain. That's why I think so many leaders get tired and worn out. It's freeing to be able to step back and say, "What are you doing, Lord? OK, if you want to do that, then show me how and send me the resource and the provision for it." And He does, if you are willing to wait for Him. Often times the Lord speaks to us, and we're all into it, and then things don't happen the way we think they should, or fast enough. So we start "helping," we start trying to move the Holy Spirit along. Then we wonder why we have to maintain something that we really don't have a lot of passion for. Remember, the Holy Spirit is a gift to us, for guidance and counseling, a gift to us that takes the pressure off.

See the freedom in that?

Following the Holy Spirit has become a thing of fear. In reality, it's freedom. His Spirit brings freedom. It's His job; He takes the burden off of us, and takes it onto Himself. All we're doing is what He is showing us.

So it's not sitting around and doing nothing. It's waiting for Him to move so we can follow. There is so much freedom in that. I've heard it said so many times, "Well, if you're not moving, then you're not doing anything." But I think we move way too much, and there is wisdom in waiting.

BLESSING THOSE WHOM GOD CHOOSES

One of the highest values John Wimber taught and lived by was the importance of seeing and blessing God's people.

John was amazing at this, because he wasn't threatened. He would see somebody, usually someone who wasn't ready for what they were doing, and he would take them, encourage them, and give them an opportunity to move forward. John gave me so much stuff that I was so not ready for! I look back now and feel sorry for those poor people...seriously.

We're called to recognize who God has His hand on, give them training, and then release them. We have to be able to let go. In the church I have seen a lot of good recruiting, a lot of good training, but not a lot of releasing.

Who really gets to play here? One of the foundations of who we are (in the Vineyard) is that everybody gets to play. John used to say it all the time! Everybody gets to play!

Some of the people playing can be scary! But it's always been that way, there is always a mix. But that should be one of our principles. We need to recognize people, even if they don't have everything together yet. Our church believes this, and I love it! Carol calls us the "anybody church." But I have to admit that I wasn't always like that. Now I love to serve the Lord, but there were days I wanted to be left alone. Somehow in my mind I justified that this was OK because I gave so many other areas of my life to ministry work, but when I went to church on Sunday... "Lord, can I please have a break?" The Lord really began to show me my heart, and it wasn't pretty.

I really didn't like many people; they had too many problems and bothered me on my day off. I thought "I give a lot of time, so can't I just come in on Sunday, get what I need, see my friends and family and go have lunch?" But I really was missing something very important, something that needed to change in me.

Years ago one of the things the Lord began to speak to me about was the power of blessing. He told me to start going to church and to change my focus. First, I needed to expect Him to move, and part of that meant that I was to begin looking for people I could bless.

If you're a leader and don't learn to bless others, then you can't expect those under you to do so. We need to create an environment where blessings are natural. God will put His hand on me for one thing, and put His hand on another for something else. He usually anoints those we often overlook. I must be able to recognize who those people are and not be threatened, but rather bless them. It's not who I pick; it's who He picks. That is who we want, because those will be the anointed ones!

That means that for me there are times when I need to step back and allow other people around me to thrive. I pray into people who are more gifted than me in different areas. I need them around me.

It seems the church has made the qualifications to "play" quite difficult for those coming in. One of the ways the Lord began to change me in this area was when He began to show me who He picked. First he picked me. That should have been enough, but He also showed me the twelve.

Remember the people Jesus placed around Him and what they were like?

Remember Matthew, tax collector, skimming money off the top? Foot-in-his-mouth Peter? John the Baptist, so full of passion, but didn't like people, and had a temper?

These are the ones Jesus chose to be with Him and to share life with Him, and these are also the people to whom Jesus entrusted, the very people for whom He came to die. He trusted them to carry on the work of the Church.

James, His brother, didn't even believe in what Jesus was doing (see John 7:3-5), yet He brought him in. How hard is it to have someone with you who doesn't really believe what you're doing, especially family? Judas, who would later betray Him, was known to embezzle money, and Jesus made him the treasurer.

There is something we're missing. These are the men Jesus let hang around Him, and to whom He chose to entrust the keys of the Kingdom.

ANOINTING OVER RESUMÉ

We tend to get in a place where we look at the qualifications, the resumé, rather than the anointing.

I'll take anointing over a resumé; people can always learn the rest. Part of following the Holy Spirit is accepting people who aren't fully mature, recognizing their calling, blessing them, training them, and releasing them. It's a privilege really.

We have people who attend our church who don't speak English, but they feel God's presence and say that's why they come. Why did so many follow Jesus during His earthly ministry? Why did the disciples leave everything when He called their name? Because they got to be with Him; they got to play!

We have *got* to let go of the lie that says if we release and bless people, we will have nothing. Remember, we give to get. Remember we only get to keep what we give away. We're called to give away our best. That's when blessing comes, and it may be a little messy, but the truth is, Kingdom work is messy.

THE GIFT OF RISK

If you and I, as followers of the One we so desire, are going to follow and seek after His leading, we should not be surprised to be taken outside of our comfort zone at least 99 percent of the time.

Ministry can be so uncomfortable at times, but it should be, it's never been about being comfortable. That's why we've been given the comforter, the Holy Spirit. We're called to risk.

So much of what John Wimber spent his life on was taking risks, and I don't mean out in the world, I mean taking risks in the church!

People don't always know how to do things the Christian way; how would they know unless we show them? We cannot expect people to come into the church and know everything right away, they will learn as they go. Of course it's important for the pastors to protect and pastor the people, but not out of fear. Leaders must be able to release people, and failure is part of that.

If the people around me aren't failing once in a while, I'm not risking enough.

The Bible tells us that Jesus believed in 12, and 11 followed after Him and changed the course of history, and one hung himself. If we give people enough rope, there will always be somebody who will hang himself. But if you focus too much on the one, you miss out on what happened with the 11.

I've received a lot of flack in the area of allowing people to participate in Kingdom work who haven't been "around long enough." Maybe someone who just came off drugs, or is having a tough time getting a job, or they don't know all our "Christian-ese." They don't seem qualified yet, but the truth is, they're already leading if people are following them. And I'm either going to take a risk and bless what I see God doing, or try and shut them down.

You can't make people follow you, at least for long, and you and I can't make people anointed. So if God obviously anoints a person for a reason, I'm either going to pastor and allow them to play or allow the fear of what could go wrong win out. If the model was good enough for Jesus, it has to be good enough for us. John used to say all the time, "We have to let the bush grow and then we trim it back."

The early Vineyard was just a bunch of young hippies; the ministry team was all young people. Yet people still got saved, healed, and delivered. God got His work done!

BEING IN TOUCH WITH THE MESSAGE

There was a reason we left the Quaker church and birthed the Vineyard. Whatever denomination you came from, whatever drew you into where you are now... there's a reason. When you walk into your church family you belong, there's something in you that makes it feel like home.

My parents felt the Vineyard was home. They left a great church, with great friends—why? For the presence of God, in a different and more tangible way then they had experienced before. It's what they didn't know they were waiting for. For all of us it's different. The reasons are different. Whatever the reasons are, I believe we have to get in touch with "what got us" over and over again.

It's important for us to remember what drew us in to wherever we are now, because whatever touched you will most likely touch the people around you.

STAYING SIMPLE

That's why staying simple is so hard. We're challenged all the time. I really believe that the Lord is taking the church back to simplicity. Love Him, love others, and allow Him to do what He wants to do. I absolutely believe that's what He's doing.

If we don't allow Him, He'll just go down the street to the local mall or bar, and find someone who will say yes to Him. One who won't feel the need to control, or allow anything else to get in the way of Him doing what He wants to do, where He wants to do it, and to whom He wants.

We do not want to get to the end of our lives and miss out on something that God had for us because it was too outside our comfort zone.

One of the things that the Lord spoke to me about being a woman in a leadership role, was, "Christy, just because it's new to you doesn't mean it's new to Me."

Another freeing thing He spoke to me was, "Christy, if people can't hear from a woman now, they won't hear from the children, and that's who I'm about to move through." I believe that with all my heart, and I'm seeing it firsthand. I'm seeing kids prophesying and having visions; and I'm telling you that what our kids see is way beyond what I've ever seen.

My daughter says, "Mom, how can you pastor and not know what this is or see it?" I don't see it, but she does!

Can we recognize what God wants? Even though we haven't experienced it, will we have eyes to see and ears to hear? Will we be able to conform and adjust?

I pray so.

Chapter Four

PARTNERING WITH JESUS IN POWER EVANGELISM

⟨◦⟩

S.J. HILL

S.J. Hill is a gifted teacher in the Body of Christ with over 38 years of experience in the ministry. He has traveled extensively, pastored, and been on the faculty of Brownsville Revival School of Ministry. He has also taught at Mike Bickle's Forerunner School of Ministry and is currently teaching part-time at F.I.R.E. School of Ministry in Concord, North Carolina. S.J. continues to travel throughout the United States and worldwide, teaching and inviting believers to a deep intimacy with their heavenly Father and His Son, Jesus Christ. His all-consuming passion is to see the Church come to an understanding of the beauty of God's incredible personality. S.J. has authored four books—*Burning Desire, Enjoying God, Personal Revival,* and *God's Covenant of Healing.*

S.J. Hill shares how you can partner with Jesus:

PARTNERSHIP

The door to the coffeehouse swung open as a wild-eyed young man staggered into the room. Disoriented and scared, he appeared to have no idea where he was. It soon became apparent that he was hallucinating on drugs and could be potentially dangerous. For the next few moments, the atmosphere in the coffeehouse was electric. Fearing that things could get out of control, several of us gathered around him and began to pray. I was deeply moved by the compassion I felt for this *stranger* who had stumbled into the room.

As we continued ministering to this young man, the power of God dramatically touched him, and he *instantly* became sober. Even those of us who had been praying for him were surprised by the sudden change we saw in him. It was as if we encountered something of *another world*! Overjoyed by what had just taken place, a couple of us attempted to explain to the young man what had happened. We talked to him about Jesus, and within minutes he gave his heart to the Lord, and his life was forever changed. When he later left the coffeehouse, he was still overwhelmed by everything that had taken place in his life that night.

As a young man in my early 20s, this experience was one of my first encounters with the supernatural. I had read about similar happenings in books written about John G. Lake, Smith Wigglesworth, and others, but I had never seen anything quite this dramatic. My faith began to grow by leaps and bounds, and I found myself living with a sense of expectation I had never known before.

Partnering With Jesus in Power Evangelism

Several months prior to this experience, I had started a Christian coffeehouse with an ex-alcoholic who had inherited some property, including a barn. This was during the time of the Jesus People Movement. The barn was very old and rustic, which added to the mystique of the place. Our motivation for starting the coffeehouse was to reach out to those in the area who normally wouldn't set foot in a church building. In fact, I'm not sure some of the churches in the surrounding communities would have been comfortable with these same individuals attending their services. Their long hair, strange dress, and coarse language would have been offensive to many. But these were the people to whom God had called us.

The barn was open most of the time, and the coffee pot was always on. People would wander in day and night, and I found myself ministering to drug dealers, those addicted to drugs and alcohol, as well as those disillusioned with life in general. I had also started several Bible studies, which added to my already busy schedule.

In the beginning, the work was extremely difficult. We not only had to deal with the unique problems that came with ministering to the "unchurched" and the "down and out," we also had to give the barn a makeover. We spent countless hours shoveling old sheep manure and pouring yards of concrete. On top of that, I was not taking a salary so that most of the money given to the ministry could be used for the renovation of the building. To say that my faith and character were being stretched in ways I had never experienced would be an understatement.

However, over time, some incredible things began to happen. Heaven invaded our coffeehouse, and the tangible power and presence of God started transforming lives. Word spread quickly about the things happening in the old barn. New converts were being added to the Kingdom on a regular basis, and I experienced a newfound joy in being allowed to partner with Jesus in ministry. I couldn't wait to see what the Lord was going to do next. Those of us who were working together continued praying that He would give us His heart for the people He would bring into our lives.

We immediately began discipling those who had come to Christ, as well as a number of other young believers. It was our desire not only to *declare* to them the realities of the Kingdom of God but also to *demonstrate* to them the power of the Kingdom.

One night a woman was brought to our Bible study who had been born with a severe birth defect. One of her legs was approximately *4 inches shorter* than the other leg. She wanted us to pray for her, so we gathered around her, and I commanded her leg to become normal in Jesus' name. Initially nothing happened; but then in an instant, her leg grew out and became as long as the other leg. Girls started screaming, and there was absolute pandemonium in the place. There was a holy awe in the room as we all sensed the presence of God in a way we had never experienced.

I later encouraged those who were present that they could expect to see the same things when they were willing to reach out to those at school or work, as well as to their friends and relatives. Over the months, it was exciting to watch these young believers turn into passionate "evangelists," sharing the Good News of what had happened to them with those around them. Although they were immature in many ways, we continually reminded them that the Lord wanted to partner with them in ministry and use them to impact the lives of others.

It wasn't long before we started hearing incredible reports of people getting saved, healed, and delivered from drugs and alcohol. The biggest drug dealer in the northern part of our state came to Christ through the witness of a couple of his friends whom I had discipled. When he was prayed for, the Holy Spirit touched him in such an overwhelming way that all he could do was pace back and forth in the field behind the coffeehouse. He couldn't even talk straight. This man went from dealing drugs to starting his own successful business. Over time, he had the privilege of leading his family and a number of his friends to the Lord.

One summer 20 individuals who had been heavy users of drugs gave their hearts to the Lord, and a number of other people switched from marijuana to Jesus. It soon became apparent that the Lord was taking "ordinary" people from all walks of life and raising them up as an army of young "radicals" to challenge the darkness in our area.

I remember the story of a man who had been powerfully saved and delivered from a life of drugs and alcohol. He had been sharing his faith with one of his closest friends who was terribly addicted to various drugs. His friend later told me that under the influence of marijuana and acid he felt he had actually left his body and had become the drum beat in one of the songs he was playing. This experience frightened him so much that he went to his buddy and asked him to pray for him to receive the Lord. With the help of several of us, he was dramatically delivered from his drug addiction and started attending our Bible studies. Both of these men became part of our ministry and had a real impact on their friends, as well as the community.

Years later while still living in the same area, I received a call from a young man who'd heard about our ministry. He had gotten involved in the occult and said he had even gone to the sixth level in witchcraft. He was in desperate need of help and wanted to know if I'd come over to his apartment and pray for him. Although he had experienced some supernatural powers, he was being tormented by demons. He could eat hardly anything and had difficulty sleeping because he said at nine o'clock every night demons would appear in his apartment.

I wasn't exactly sure what to expect when I went to visit him one evening, but I knew the Lord had given me authority over all the powers of darkness. As I was sitting in his living room talking to him about his need for the Lord, I heard footsteps on his balcony. They were so real that I got up from the sofa and opened the door to see who was there. At that point, the young man said to me, "It's nine o'clock, and they're here." I thought to myself, *Who's he talking about?* Then I remembered what he had told me, and I braced myself for what would happen next.

I sat back on the sofa and immediately heard footsteps in the bedroom, with doors opening and closing at the same time. I had heard of poltergeists (noisy ghosts), but I had never experienced anything like this. Without getting off the couch, I turned in the direction of the noise and commanded it to stop in the name of Jesus. The demonic activity in the bedroom immediately stopped, and to my knowledge the young man was never tormented again. Eventually he gave his heart to the Lord, and his life was completely turned around.

Stories like the ones I've shared became commonplace. I watched as the Kingdom of God advanced in our community, and I loved being a small part of it. Looking back and reflecting on what began in the early days of our coffeehouse ministry, I'm even more convinced today that what we've since seen and experienced over the years is what *normal* Christianity should be.

WE ARE ALL CALLED TO MINISTRY

I believe one of the things the Holy Spirit is restoring in this hour is a call to the Christian community to both *declare* and *demonstrate* the Good News of the Kingdom of God in the market-place. It's an invitation from the heart of God to partner with Him in *friendship evangelism*. But in order for us as believers to be released into ministry and to embrace the call the Lord has for each one of us, several prevalent mindsets will need to be changed.

First of all, if we want to experience the power of the gospel in our lives, we need to eliminate from our thinking the religious distinction between a professional "clergy" and a "laity," something that was conceived by man and not God. This is absolutely neces-sary since the word *clergy* is never used in Scripture with reference to those who have been called to function in any of the five ministry gifts of Ephesians 4:11. The Greek term from which the word *clergy* originates occurs only once in the New Testament (1 Pet. 5:3), and there it's used to describe the congregation of people and not the pastor or elder. In this passage, Peter admonishes the elders not to act as "lords over God's heritage." The word "heritage" is the Greek term *kleros* from which the word *clergy* is derived. This word came to be applied to the fivefold ministry gifts because the elders disregarded Peter's instruction and began to consider themselves God's special *heritage*, like the priests and Levites of the Old Testament. Although the New Testament applies the term *heritage* or *clergy* to the congregation of believers, eventually the elders applied the term exclusively to themselves.

Another reason why the terms *clergy* and *laity* should be eliminated from our thinking and vocabulary is because the word *laity* is a term used today to describe those who don't *appear* to be in "full-time ministry" as opposed to those who are engaged in some form of religious work. The word *laity* is from the Greek word *laos*, meaning "people." The term appears in First Peter 2:9, and here the *laity* are called the "royal priesthood." It should be obvious that if the Word of God refers to all believers as God's *clergy* and *priesthood*, then there should be no ecclesiastical distinctions in the Body of Christ. *While some individuals are given ministry gifts of leadership for the purpose of equipping the saints for service, every one of us has a ministry to perform and has been given gifts to fulfill the destiny the Lord has for us* (see Eph. 4:11-12). The differences are strictly functional.

In the New Testament, the *laity* were not merely "spectators" to whom the *clergy* preached. The people of God didn't employ others to evangelize for them, cast out demons for them, or pray for the sick on their behalf. In the early Church all the believers spread the gospel and ministered to the needs of those around them. They knew this was their calling as much as it was the calling of their leaders, regardless of what their regular employment may have been.

In Acts 8:1-4, we're told that *ordinary* disciples were scattered throughout the regions and "...went everywhere preaching the word," while the apostles remained in Jerusalem. Later, God didn't send a prophet or apostle to Paul after his conversion on the road to Damascus; instead, we're told that it was "...*a certain disciple* at Damascus named Ananias" who was sent to lay hands on Paul so he might receive his sight and be filled with the Spirit (Acts 9:10-12,17).

Within a few years after Christ had given the Great Commission to the Church, the early Christians had spread the gospel throughout much of the world. This was accomplished without any of the modern-day technology or advanced methods of communication. There were no printed Bibles or Christian literature. Methods of travel were slow and tedious, and there were very few adequate roads. But even without all the modern methods of travel and communication, they were able to experience the supernatural realities of the Kingdom of God because they knew they were called to partner with the Lord in ministry.

According to Mark 16:16-18, Jesus had promised that certain *signs* would follow every believer. These *signs* were not meant to merely follow the apostles, pastors, or evangelists. The Lord used many other believers to preach, work miracles, cast out demons, and heal the sick. Stephen, Philip, and Ananias were not apostles, and yet they were used significantly in the work of the ministry.

What we need today is not more people giving up their jobs, dedicating their lives to "full-time Christian service," and seeking some form of religious employment; what is needed is for all of us as Christians to become full-time disciples of Jesus, witnessing and ministering within the realm of life and employment we now find ourselves. What we could do in any other place or circumstance, we can do right now where we are. We can share our faith, pray for the sick and those in need, liberate the demonically oppressed, and serve our neighbor in love.

Second, if we expect to experience the power of God in the

marketplace, we need to rid ourselves of the unscriptural idea that the local church is meant to be the "center of evangelism." To some degree, the Commission given by Jesus to "Go" into the world and make disciples by evangelizing the lost has been replaced by the message, "Come to church, and let the pastor evangelize you from the pulpit."

Although I'm all for inviting the unsaved to meetings with the purpose of seeing them come to Christ, the Church, by its very nature, is made up of born-again believers who gather together around the Person of Jesus Christ for worship, fellowship, the celebrating of the ordinances, and the study of Scriptures. In fact, the language in First Corinthians 14:23-25 clearly suggests that for unbelievers to be present in a service is not the norm, but rather an exception to the rule.

Since much of the emphasis in our services consists largely of evangelistic appeals to the audience, Christians are not being properly trained to do the work of the ministry in the marketplace. Because of a lack of teaching, many of them now assume that the work of evangelism is primarily the responsibility of the pastor on Sunday or the evangelist who is invited each year to "hold revival meetings." As a result, a large number of believers today have become bored and unfruitful.

Is it any wonder that far too many Christians no longer consider the communication and demonstration of the Good News their *primary* calling and privilege? The tragedy is that they have become, for all intents and purposes, mere spectators who are convinced that they fulfill their God-given responsibilities by attending services and giving financial support to a professional clergy whom they employ to function spiritually on their behalf.

Third, in order for us to partner with Jesus in power evangelism, we need to realize that it has been a mistake to think that our work or profession is not Christian because it's not within the context of a church or religious organization. There is no biblical basis whatsoever for the ecclesiastical distinction between "spiritual" work and so-called "secular" work. The Bible never speaks of "secular employment" to describe work outside the sphere of the Church. This idea has robbed many of us of the primary purpose of our calling, which is to live our lives as disciples of Christ and minister to those within our field of employment. We, as Christians, are called to serve the Lord faithfully wherever we are.

MARKETPLACE CHRISTIANITY

As I've already mentioned, over the years an unbiblical concept has emerged concerning Christian vocation and calling. A distinction was developed between *laity* (ordinary laymen of whom little was expected spiritually and whose work was designated as "secular") and *clergy* (made up of full-time religious workers whose activity was called Christian). As a result of this erroneous distinction, if our work is outside a church or parachurch context, our "calling" means little more than how we earn money to pay our bills. Regardless of how noble the work or profession is in providing a real service to our fellowman, it is nevertheless considered "secular" in nature.

On the other hand, "Christian" vocation and calling have taken on an ecclesiastical connotation meaning the dedication of one's life to full-time Christian service, or employment by some church or religious organization. Furthermore, such work is considered "spiritual" even though it may consist of working as a secretary in a church office, or volunteering to collect clothes or donations for some religious organization on behalf of the poor.

To further illustrate the fallacy of such an idea, imagine a Christian doctor who works as a surgeon in a prominent hospital. Although he may treat the sick in a very godly, compassionate way and even pray for his patients before he operates on them, under the prevailing idea of what constitutes Christian calling and vocation, he would be considered a "layman" and his profession classified as "secular."

However, if the same doctor believed he was called to a foreign field and he was ultimately sent out by a mission's board, his medical practice would then somehow be considered "spiritual," and he would be recognized as a missionary. We can only imagine what the apostle Paul would have said about these unscriptural distinctions since he made tents while he preached the Word of God, never calling his tent-making "secular" work and his preaching "spiritual" service.

The Bible clearly indicates that God calls all believers to full-time Christian service from the moment they're saved. Every person who is converted to Christ is given a *calling*. This is reinforced for us in Ephesians 4:1, where Paul addressed all of the disciples in the Church in Ephesus, saying, "I, therefore, the prisoner of the Lord, beseech you to walk worthy of the calling with which you were called." Whatever our role may be in life or the nature of our employment after we're saved, we are informed in First Corinthians 7:24 that such is God's calling for us. The idea that in order to be involved in Christian service we must quit our jobs and seek employment in some religious organization or church is clearly refuted by the previous verse.

Therefore it's imperative we understand that all work is "spiritual" if there is a Christian in it, it glorifies God, and it serves one's fellowman in love. Work has real dignity in God's sight, whether employed in a factory or office, or whether a businessperson, farmer, or stay-at-home mom. As Christians, our present employment or sphere of influence is "spiritual" because we have been called by God to take His Kingdom with us wherever we go, touching people's lives in the process.

I have a very close friend who works in real estate on the island of Kauai. He also shapes and repairs surfboards. One day Scott was coming in from surfing Hanalei Bay on the north shore of the island, and he saw a friend whose board he had recently repaired. This man was discreetly smoking a joint on Hanalei Pier, trying to get high.

Scott went over to his friend and discovered that his "buzzed buddy" had recently injured his elbow and couldn't bend it. The guy was bummed out because he hadn't been able to work for some time. Scott began telling him stories of people he had seen healed through the power of the name of Jesus. He told the man about a friend of his whose left wrist had been operated on a number of years ago. The doctors had put a steel plate in his wrist that was held in place by nine bolts. He had not been able to bend his wrist for 19 years. He wanted to play the guitar but was unable because of the surgery. Scott asked him if he could pray for him, and after prayer he immediately was able to bend his wrist in spite of the steel plate and nine bolts.

Scott continued telling healing stories to his surfing buddy, and then asked him if he could pray for him. Initially, his friend wouldn't let him. But after talking to him a little longer, Scott asked him how his elbow was feeling. The man admitted that he was in a lot of pain, but he still didn't ask for prayer. Without hesitation, Scott said, "Father, in Jesus' name, heal my friend's elbow." He then looked at his buddy and said, "Bend it and check it out." All the man could say was, "Wow, this is weird," as he moved his elbow back and forth.

Scott saw his friend at the beach a few days later, and he asked him how he was doing. The man said he was back to work framing houses and swinging a hammer again without any pain. Think of it—the Lord used a Christian Realtor who loves surfing to bring healing to a man who was smoking a joint. Jesus is still the friend of sinners!

On another occasion, Scott was in a restaurant eating lunch with his wife and a couple of their friends. Their server was an older woman who showed signs of having experienced a difficult life. She was wearing Velcro casts on her forearms and wrists. Scott had a strong impression that the Lord wanted him to pray for this woman. After some small talk and joking with her, Scott asked her if she had

Carpal Tunnel Syndrome in her wrists. She said, "Yes, I do. I can barely lift the plates and do my job." Someone at the table suggested that they pray for her, so Scott asked the server if that would be OK. Although somewhat reluctant, she said, "I guess so." Scott then led out in a simple prayer for healing and encouraged her to believe that Jesus would touch her.

A couple of weeks later Scott and his wife came back to the restaurant and saw the server for whom they had prayed. It appeared that there were no Velcro casts on her forearms and wrists. When she saw Scott and his wife, she threw her arms in the air and in front of a number of other people, she blurted out, "Jesus healed me of Carpal Tunnel Syndrome. Jesus healed me of Carpal Tunnel Syndrome!" With tears in her eyes and her voice quivering, she later told Scott and his wife, "Now I know Jesus is real and that He loves me!"

CELEBRATING THE KINGDOM OF GOD

Shortly after the birth of Christ, an angel appeared to shepherds and gladly proclaimed, "I bring you good news that will bring great joy to all people" (Luke 2:10 NLT). At the heart of the gospel message is a call to celebrate a Savior who has taken away the sins of the world; it's a call to embrace the God who reconciled the world to Himself!

This was the message of the early Christians that stood out in stark contrast to the prevailing thought of the religions of their day. In the Roman world, you couldn't count on the gods being for you. They were unpredictable and unreliable. But the message of the gospel was such good news that the first Christians couldn't keep it to themselves—"God died and rose again because He loves you and He's for you!" It was a message that was truly for everyone. In Christ, social distinctions became irrelevant. Everyone had equal worth and dignity in the eyes of God. Is it any wonder that Christianity turned the world upside down?

This is the Good News that we've also been called to take with us into every arena of life. We've been entrusted with the "ministry of reconciliation" (2 Cor. 5:18-20), not the message of "turn or burn." Many of our methods of evangelism are far too impersonal. People are not "trophies" we mount on our walls. This is why it's *imperative* that we properly represent the Lord wherever we go. The Kingdom of God is meant to be *celebrated!* He has given us the privilege of sharing with others the incredible story of His desire to introduce them to His Father so they can be a part of His family.

GOOD NEWS FOR ALL

I was recently sent an e-mail from a friend of mine who is part of our local church. One afternoon, Joel, along with several other Christian businessmen, went into a very rough neighborhood to reach out with the love of Jesus Christ to those in the community. As things were winding down that evening, someone came running up to the men and asked them for help to find a 7-year-old boy who had disappeared in the neighborhood. Together they began to pray that God would show them where the boy was. One of the men felt the Lord told him that the boy was sound asleep in the back seat of his mom's car. When they found the boy's mother, she was hysterical. Although she felt it was impossible for her son to be in her car, she proceeded to show the men where her car was. When they got to the vehicle and looked inside, the boy was there, asleep on the back seat.

Later that evening, a man wearing dark sunglasses was introduced to my friend. The man explained that four years earlier he had been involved in a chemical explosion in a closed trailer, and ammonium-chloride had blown up in his face. He said he was practically blind as a result. The doctors had sewn his eyes shut for seven months and any exposure to light caused excruciating pain. This is why he had to wear dark sunglasses even at night. He also shared that the chemicals had burned all the color out of his irises and that before the accident his eyes had been dark brown in color.

Joel then proceeded to tell him that he had "good news" for him: Jesus wanted to heal his eyes and restore his sight. Several of the men present began to pray for the man, and his eyes started to water. What the men didn't realize was that his eyes hadn't watered in four years. The man was smiling from ear to ear as he said, "I can see a little bit; I can see a little bit. My wife is going to freak out! I can see a little bit." But his eyes still looked milky-gray in color. My friend then proceeded to lay hands on the man again and pray for him a second time. When he took his hands off the man's eyes, the man began to jump, shouting, "I can see. I can see!" One of the other men began to scream. He jumped back and grabbed my friend's shoulders. "Joel, I just saw a miracle! I just watched the color come back into the guy's eyes."

This miracle triggered a series of events resulting in a number of other people getting healed as well. Before the day was over, approximately 40 people had given their hearts to the Lord. The Kingdom of God had come to an impoverished neighborhood through a group of Christian businessmen, and lives would never be the same.

Some of what I've shared in this chapter may be a bit over-whelming for some of you. It may be hard for you to imagine God using you in any significant way. You may feel completely unqualified to minister in the marketplace. You may even be somewhat introverted and shy. But I want to encourage you to remember that it's the Lord's desire to partner with you in ministry.

You're His unique, one-of-a-kind son or daughter, and He loves being with you. He wants to use you more than you realize so that you can enter into the celebration of His Kingdom. Start expecting Him to bring people across your path. Trust Him to give you words of information and encouragement for them. All He expects of you is that you allow Him to touch the lives of the people around you by befriending them, loving them, taking time to listen to them, and being open to praying for them.

Personally, the more I've understood how much Father likes me and enjoys being with me, the more I've gone from trying to witness out of religious duty and obligation to wanting to share the Father's love with others. I've thoroughly enjoyed talking to people on airplanes, in malls and restaurants, and many other places about the concept of "enjoying God," and then watching them respond as they realized God wanted to be their Father and that He was nothing like the angry, vindictive God that "religion" had made Him out to be.

Some of my fondest memories took place in a fitness center where the owner and others gave their hearts to the Lord. I loved going outside the "church structure," discipling these new believers and seeing the power of God change their lives. I was even asked to pray for a couple of young men for deliverance from "roid rage" because of all the steroids they had used, and the Lord powerfully touched them and set them free. And we did this in the only private place available—the sauna!

God is calling each of you to be a pied piper, leading this generation into the celebration of the Good News of the Kingdom. Your life is not insignificant. You have a sphere of influence no one else has.

Please join me in partnering with Jesus in power evangelism. It's time to celebrate!

Chapter 5

GAINING THE GAZE OF GOD

∞

BOBBY CONNER

B obby Conner has an extensive ministry background as a Southern Baptist pastor, and he ministers in a high level, proven prophetic anointing. He believes his calling is to equip the Body of Christ to hear and discern God's voice in these times. He is well-loved and best known the world over for his sensitivity to and leading of the Holy Spirit. Highly esteemed as an internationally acclaimed conference speaker, Bobby has ministered effectively to more than 45 foreign countries as well as in the United States for many years. Bobby has been ministering for more than 38 years, and averages speaking five times a week.

Bobby Conner provides insights about how you can gain the gaze of God:

IN WHOM I AM WELL-PLEASED

Nothing could be more satisfying than knowing that your life is pleasing to God and hearing, "This is my beloved child in whom I am well pleased!"

The Lord is looking for a people whose heart is upright with Him, so that He can fully support all that they are doing see (see 2 Chron. 16:9). The Spirit of Truth is raising up leaders that will teach the people the vast difference between what is pure and what is profane (see Ezek. 44:23). It is crucial that we walk in uprightness if we are to ascend the hill of the Lord (see Ps. 24:3-4). It is very important that we do whatever needs to be done to walk in true authority. However, there is something more needful than just *ascending* into the hill of the Lord—that is *abiding* in the hill or presence of the Lord (see Ps. 15:1).

The Body of Christ must advance from just visitation to habitation (see Eph. 2:20-22). It is one thing to display the *power of God* but is so much better to reveal the *person of Christ*. As we embrace accountability, we can then be trusted with more true authority. Christ Jesus informed us that if we are faithful over little, we will become ruler over much more (see Matt. 25:14-21). On the other hand, if we fail to handle small things correctly, even the small things are in danger of being removed (see Matt. 25:24-29). It is required of a steward that he be found faithful (see 1 Cor. 4:2). Our goal is to live in such a manner that when we stand before the Lord He will say well done good and faithful servant. These days call for the highest standard of leadership.

The message of the Book of Jude is blasting out to this end-time Church age. The warning is all too clear: if we do not return to the acts of the apostles, we will continue to see the actions of the apostates. It is imperative that we become contenders and defenders of the faith, and "...contend for the faith that was once for all entrusted to the saints" (Jude 3).

In a vivid prophetic experience the Spirit of the Lord spoke these encouraging words to me, *"Accept no imitations! Expect no limitations! Embrace infinite possibilities!"* As we aspire to make these three areas a living reality in our lives, we will see the Church being launched into a much higher level.

ACCEPT NO IMITATIONS

Artificial, counterfeit, synthetic—these are but a few words that help us grasp a better understanding of the word *imitation*. I once asked the president of a leading bank, "How do your tellers detect a counterfeit bill?" His answer was profound, "The best way to expose phony money is to have someone who is so accustomed to handling the real thing that when they touch a fake, something within them instantly sets off a warning."

This is what the Body of Christ must have: true intimacy with Jesus that instantly reveals any imitation. We must become so accustomed to His voice that we are not moved by the enticing of a stranger's voice. If we are the sheep of His fold, we must come to know His voice, and follow the voice of our Shepherd. We cannot continue to spend our lives on that which is worthless. Everything that is wood, hay, and stubble must be removed from our Christian walk.

It is crucial for the Church to commence walking in true apostolic authority. However, if we are going to be trusted with a higher level of authority it is essential for us to walk in integrity and uprightness. The writer of the Book of Hebrews instructs us to pursue peace as well as purity for without it we will not see the Lord.

The Lord spoke these encouraging words to me, *"If I can find a people without mixture, I will pour out My power without measure."*

According to the Book of Revelation, there will emerge a group of "overcomers" walking in true Kingdom power. This causes three questions to arise in my heart: *If not you, who? If not here, where? If not now, when?*

THE ZADOK PRIESTHOOD

I was recently in the Northwest region of the United States and it suddenly began to rain the most wonderful sweet, steady rain seemingly from a cloudless sky. I asked the Lord, "What is this rain a sign of?" In response, I heard within my spirit, *"The substantial rainfall signified the anointed teaching that is being released through the emerging Zadok priesthood."* These anointed priests will begin to authenticate that which is holy and expose that which is profane. This is what the Lord called the Zadok priesthood to do: "Moreover, they shall teach My people the difference between the holy and the profane, and cause them to discern between the unclean and the clean" (Ezek. 44:23 NASB). What is the difference between the profane and the holy? The Lord said what He called profane was anything we are doing that He did not initiate. Remember the words of Christ Jesus when He states, "I never knew you, depart from Me you who practice lawlessness" (Matt. 7:23). These words were spoken to a person who had been very involved in religious activity, but did not truly trust Christ.

The fundamental purpose of the Zadok priesthood is to minister to the Lord as described in Ezekiel 44:15-16:

> *"But the priests, the Levites, the sons of Zadok, who kept charge of My sanctuary when the children of Israel went astray from Me, they shall come near Me to minister to Me; and they shall stand before Me to offer Me the fat and the blood," says the Lord God. "They shall enter*

My sanctuary, and they shall come near My table to minister to Me, and they shall keep My charge."

This signifies an emphasis on the fivefold ministry of prophetic teachers as they prepare the Body of Christ to receive the strong prophetic and apostolic ministries yet to be truly inaugurated.

TEACHING THE TRUTH

The Spirit of Truth is seeking to establish each one of us in truth. Christ Jesus commanded, "Sanctify them by Your truth; Your word is truth" (John 17:17). As believers, we are to have upright lives which are characterized by authentic lifestyles of faith. Our walk must match our talk if we are to have a message that will legitimately change lives. It is time to take a stand for righteousness and holiness.

Grace is not a license to live loose. In our attempts to appear politically correct, have we drifted far from the calling to stand for truth and righteousness? Only as we return to true holiness of heart can we be vessels of honor. This will allow us to be sanctified in truth and be presentable to the Lord as consecrated vessels. The call is clear. We must present the truth in order for true freedom to reign in our hearts. God is calling each of us to embrace the conditions of Second Corinthians 7:1, "Therefore, having these promises, beloved, let us cleanse ourselves from all filthiness of the flesh and spirit, perfecting holiness in the fear of God."

Many feel a sense of disorientation at this time; this is the result of being upon the "Potter's wheel." However, be assured the Master Potter Himself is about to touch the soft pliable clay, and soon we will bear His image. We are in a time of transition that will produce transformation. Our responsibility is to remain soft and moist—yielded upon the Master's wheel. If we attempt to mold ourselves or if we allow ourselves to become dry and brittle we must be broken and remolded. It is imperative that we stay soft and surrendered before the Lord.

CHARACTER—NOT JUST GIFTINGS

Presently these emerging leaders are in a season of sifting and pruning—the refiner's fire is forging their character to carry this unique anointing. They will be the leaders and counselors who will not judge by what their eyes see nor what their ears hear, but in true righteousness they will make decisions resulting in equity and justice.

The refiner's fire is absolutely purifying these leaders so the anointing will not be lost nor the wineskins damaged or destroyed for lack of character. It will be a true impartation of the divine nature and holy character established in the spirit and soul of the Lord's leadership.

As our character is formed upon the Potter's wheel and through the Refiner's fire, it is imperative that we do not forget the wonderful promise given by the Spirit of God, *"If I can find a people without mixture, I will pour out My power without measure."* Again, let me impress upon each of us the mandate to embrace the promise of purity found in Second Corinthians 7:1, "Therefore, having these promises, beloved, let us cleanse ourselves from all filthiness of the flesh and spirit, perfecting holiness in the fear of God." The results of this embrace will be the identifying of us as sons and daughters of the almighty God. What an awesome motivation for purity.

The Spirit of Truth is calling for each of us to walk as did the true Zadok priests. These priests had the responsibility of modeling and maintaining the highest standards of morality, self-control, and self-denial. They were charged with the ministry of teaching the people how to distinguish between what was godly and ungodly, so no deception would lead the people away from the Lord.

We must remember that there is a vast difference between deception and denial. Many today are actually walking in deception because they do not know that they have departed from the true path of righteousness. Those who embrace the call to the Zadok priesthood will be used by God to unveil their deception. However, many are also aware of their wanderings, but choose to walk in denial of the fact that they have turned away from their first love. Only those who deal with any and every way that their allegiance to Christ is artificial, and become genuine, authentic, and unadulterated in their walk with Him will inherit the powerful and precious promises God is pouring out to His end-times Church.

EXPECT NO LIMITATIONS

In Scripture the question is posed, "Is there anything too hard for the Lord?" (Gen. 18:14). The prophet Jeremiah answers this question clearly: "Ah, Lord God! Behold, You have made the heavens and the earth by Your great power and outstretched arm. There is nothing too hard for You" (Jer. 32:17). The cry of our soul must be: "God, nothing is impossible with You!" If we would expect more, I am sure God would release more. According unto your faith be it unto you. Let's pray for big faith that moves the hand of God. Now is the time to think big, God can do anything. It is time to expect more, believe for more, and ask for more. Paul the apostle reminded us that, God "is able to do exceeding abundantly above all we could ask or think according to the power that works in us" (Eph. 3:20-21).

The following are some faith-building statements from saints of yesterday:

> There are boundless possibilities for us, if we dare to
> act in God and dare to believe.
> —SMITH WIGGLESWORTH

> The only limit to the power of God lies within the
> individual.
> —KATHRYN KUHLMAN

It is when active faith dares to believe God to the point of action that something has to happen.

—KATHRYN KUHLMAN

EMBRACE INFINITE POSSIBILITIES

In order to embrace someone we must seek to draw near, reaching forth our hand, taking hold of them, and bringing them near to our heart. A true embrace is heart to heart; there is no such thing as a distant embrace. We cannot embrace this coming move of God from a distance. He is calling each of us to draw nearer to Him. It is time to come aside to know His heart. In Psalm 46:10 we are instructed to be still and know that He is the Lord. It is only as we behold His face that we are truly changed into His divine image. So I encourage you to meditate upon these promises. If we will accept no imitation and walk in unadulterated union with Christ, all the while seeking to have an indisputable relationship with Christ Jesus, then we can expect no limitations. It is time now to begin to embrace the formation of a character within us that will release God's infinite possibilities.

As believers we are instructed to live our daily lives with true goals, aims, and divine purpose. We cannot achieve this unless we walk in God's grace.

God is not looking for strong people to help Him accomplish His work. The Lord is looking for people who are weak enough to be used. We must remember that His strength is made perfect in our weakness (see 2 Cor. 12:9). The key to experiencing supernatural liberating strength is personal weakness. Now let me make it clear that I am not speaking about weak character, or being weak in knowing the Scriptures. I am talking about a people who have come to the place where they have lost confidence in the power of the flesh to accomplish the work of the Spirit. It is at this point when we become strong and "graced" to accomplish things for the true advancing of God's glorious Kingdom.

This truth is clearly displayed in the story found in Psalm 107:23-28 of the strong, seaworthy sailors who made their living upon the high seas. However, one day the Lord raised up a stormy wind that blew away all their self-confidence. They found themselves at their wit's end. It was at this point that they cried out for the Lord's grace and help. Though they were skilled and experienced, the winds and waves of the sea convinced them of their dependence upon God. Have you encountered the winds of change in your life? If not, you can be confident they are on their way, in order to test your foundation.

Christ Jesus declares "without Me you can accomplish nothing!" (John 15:5). The word *nothing* means: "completely, totally nothing." It truly means less than nothing. It is a life of joy when we come to the place where we understand that it must be the work of the Spirit to advance the Kingdom of God.

Absolutely nothing you have ever done, nothing you could ever accomplish, will match the unparalleled joy of allowing Jesus to live His life through you. God has exactly fitted for each of us a unique walk of grace. As we yield our wills and ways to the control of God's Holy Spirit, we begin to experience the walk of grace. In this arena, you will experience the abundant grace that enables you to accomplish all that God has assigned you to do.

This deposit of grace is what makes the fire of passion burn so brightly in new believers. One of the great joys of pastoring people for years was the overwhelming joy of watching a new believer express with excitement the new things God was doing in their lives. The joy and excitement of new believers are contagious. It is extremely refreshing to be around brand-new believers; their entire life is ablaze with the love of God. As pastor, I was able to teach a new converts' class, and my heart was always blessed by the joy that Jesus Christ produced in the life of a new believer. It is this grace that causes the light of contentment to dance in the eyes of mature believers who have learned the secret of walking the grace walk. Our lives should testify to the ability of God's awesome grace to use us to accomplish great and mighty things for the glory of God.

You cannot separate life's actions from a grace-filled life. We are saved by grace, and we are kept by God's awesome grace. The Body of Christ seems to understand much concerning the grace of God touching an unbeliever's life, and bringing that person into a place of salvation. However, we lack true understanding concerning the ability of God's grace to operate in the daily lives of believers, thereby bringing them into a place of true effectiveness and fruitfulness. Grace does not just change your mind. It has a transforming effect upon your life. Grace is a powerful motivator provoking us to reach higher and accomplish more for Christ and His Kingdom.

ESSENTIAL INGREDIENTS FOR GRACE

The apostle Paul stated in First Corinthians 15:10, "But by the grace of God I am what I am, and His grace toward me was not in vain; but I labored more abundantly than they all, yet not I, but the grace of God which was with me." Paul declared that the grace of God was not wasted upon his life, but he labored more because of the grace active in his life. Though all we are and all we do are because of God's grace, we are still called to labor abundantly to advance His Kingdom. One of the great paradoxes of the Christian life is that it is only by and through grace that we accomplish anything, yet God expects us to labor diligently in His service. Charles Spurgeon said, *"Faith goes up the stairs that love has built and looks out the window which hope has opened."*

Just as diligent labor is required to extract out all of the grace that God has given us, humility is required to obtain grace. "All of you, clothe yourselves with humility toward one another, because, 'God opposes the proud, but gives grace to the humble'" (1 Pet. 5:5 NASB). Grace is promised to the humble. A great saint of years by gone, Walter Buettler, made this observation—*"the moment humility announces herself she is already on her way out the door."* If we would be truly humble, and careful not to touch the glory of God, always giving Him praise for what He is doing, I am sure we would receive more grace. The Lord warned me once that the highest form of treason was to take the gifts and graces He has given leadership to win and woo the Bride to Himself, and then use these gifts and graces to win the Bride to ourselves.

May each heart embrace the promise given in Psalm 84:11 (NASB), "For the Lord God is a sun and shield; the Lord gives grace and glory...." In this passage we see the true key to the advancing of the Kingdom of God. It is by God's gift of grace that we are able to behold the glory. Any good thing ever accomplished by humankind is the direct result of the anointing and impartation of God's grace. May we walk a grace-filled life in order to see the glory of God fill the earth.

Grace is an open door that bids us to draw nearer to God. In Proverbs 8:17,21, God declares, "I love those who love Me, and those who seek Me diligently will find Me.... That I may cause those who love Me to inherit wealth, that I may fill their treasuries." Now this is an awesome promise and powerful incentive, finding God and having Him bless us with overflowing treasures. We must never forget that God has great plans for His people. Hear His promise in Jeremiah 29:11, "For I know the thoughts that I think toward you, says the Lord, thoughts of peace, and not of evil, to give you a future and a hope." It is time to open our hearts wide to the grace of God. He is a good God and has great plans for each of us.

WAITING UPON GOD

The Lord desires to change us. He seeks to bring us up into His purpose for us. He waits for us to reach out to Him and knock on the door of His heart. Just as Esther had to approach the throne of her husband, we too must prepare ourselves to approach the throne of God. He, too, has extended His scepter. Now is the time grace has provided an open door in Heaven. It is time to approach the throne of God's grace to find favor and help during these days.

Spending quiet time in the Lord's presence is tremendous, and carries great importance. It is as we wait upon Him that we are renewed in power and strength (see Isa. 40:28-31). Each of us must find a special quiet place where we can shut out the cares of this world and get alone with God. Each day we should come within our "set apart place" to worship, acknowledge His goodness and grace concerning us, and thank Him for His guidance and blessing upon our lives. Great grace is released when we truly enter His gates with thanksgiving and into His courts with praise by taking the time to praise the Lord and to bless His holy name.

As we take time to behold Him with an unveiled face, we are changed into ever-increasing glory. In this place of quiet worship and prayerful reading of His holy Word, there is a release of grace producing "Spirit and Life" which flows into our being to build our faith and provide the "enabling grace" for obedience. It is essential that we set apart time each day to be in His presence. Being part of a local church and attending church services are essential and not to be neglected, but this is no substitute for our devotional times alone with the Lord of glory.

BEING ONE WITH THE LORD

Notice in Luke 3:2 that the Word of God came to John while he was alone in the wilderness. The programs of the "church" of that day were in full operation, yet John was called apart to be with the Lord alone. So also today, there are those who are spiritually hungry and seeking something more, who likewise are being called apart to be alone with the Lord for a time of preparation. As a result of his being alone with the Lord, John came into a oneness with the Lord that could not have been accomplished in any other way.

When John was asked who he was, his response testifies to this experience. He said, "I am the voice of one crying in the wilderness 'Make straight the way of the Lord,' as the prophet Isaiah said" (John 1:23). Each one of us should come to the place where we also could make this statement: "I am the voice of One." There is an urgent need for this "voice" to cry out in the midst of the frustrations and perils of our present day. We live in a world that must have the grace and peace of God.

The need today is not newfangled methodology, but rather a turning aside to stand in the manifest presence of the Lord to be prepared as "the voice of one crying in the wilderness" of our day. May it be stated of us, as it was of the disciples of old, that it is apparent that we have been with Jesus. This and only this will make the changes that must occur if we are to reach this hurting world with the message of God's redemptive transforming grace.

Toward the end of his life, a popular minister was asked what he would do if he had his life to live over again. He said he had spent seven years in preparation for 45 years of ministry. Instead, he would spend 45 years in preparation for seven years of ministry. It is very important how we begin, but it is far more important how we end.

The Lord is seeking to bring us to the end of our abilities so we can tap into His ability. This requires that we recognize His presence and turn aside to stand before Him. Only then will we become the expression of His voice—crying in the wilderness of our day.

GOD VALUES YOUR FRIENDSHIP

The world we live in is extremely fast paced. Computers, iPods, cell phones, voice mail, e-mail, instant messaging, and other high-tech gadgets seem to leave very little opportunity for really getting to know people and developing true, lasting friendships.

In our busy world it is tragic to admit that many times it is the most important of these relationships, our companionship with Christ, that suffers the most. The Spirit of God calls each of us to turn aside from the cares and chaos of this world and come to Him for true companionship and friendship.

MAINTAINING TRUE FRIENDSHIP

As followers of Christ, even in the midst of a civilization that seems to shun true friendship we must never forget that we have a true Friend in "high places." This true Friend is the Son of God, Christ the Lord. He is a True Friend that remains closer than a brother. We could have no higher position than to be known as a true friend of God.

The most contented people in the world are those who have found Jesus Christ to be life's truest Friend. A true friend is one who is always there for you. You can confide the deepest secrets of your heart with a dear, trusted friend. God also shares His secrets with His trusted Friends. Jesus promised in John 15:15: "No longer do I call you servants, for a servant does not know what his master is doing; but I have called you friends, for all things that I heard from My Father I have made known to you." The happiest people on earth are those who have surrendered control of their lives to the Spirit of God and entered into this friendship. The songwriter of old said it well, "What a friend we have in Jesus…"!

VALUE AND WORTH

God Himself highly values not only His friendship with you, but you His friend. The Lord has ascribed to you great worth. Countless numbers of Christians have never stopped to ponder the great value that God has placed upon their lives. It is almost overwhelming to consider the fact that almighty God has chosen you to become the eternal companion of His dear Son!

Can you imagine that, with the entire universe under His control and care, Father God actually delights and takes pleasure in fellowshipping with you? Truly you are extremely special to God. Knowing this, you should never be plagued with thoughts of unworthiness, feeling that your life has no true meaning or purpose. Christ would have done all that He did in coming to earth and dying on the cross if you were the only one on earth that needed redemption. That is how special you are to God! Heaven places great worth and value upon you. You are incredibly special to God.

How do we ascertain what something is worth? What determines the value of something? The answer: what someone is willing to pay for it. Think about it. God was willing to give Heaven's best—His own Son—to redeem you. That shows your true worth and reveals your eternal value. Never again allow the enemy to make you feel like you don't have any real worth.

The Creator of the entire universe desires that you be in His presence for all eternity. There is no need to suffer in despair and loneliness when Christ reaches out to each of us and offers true love and friendship.

LIVING WITH PURPOSE—NOT STARDOM

As we daily continue walking in friendship and union with Christ, Scripture states that we walk in the light as He is in the light, and we have fellowship with one another. "But if we walk in the light as He is in the light, we have fellowship with one another, and the blood of Jesus Christ His Son cleanses us from all sin" (1 John 1:7). This is where our cleansing, contentment, and comradeship stem from: union with Christ. As we abide in Him, our life finds its purpose and pleasure.

The most confident people on the face of the earth are Christians who are totally yielded to the control of the Spirit of God. Knowing that God has good plans for our lives, we are called to be living with a divine goal, aim, and purpose. "See then that you walk circumspectly, not as fools but as wise, redeeming the time, because the days are evil. Therefore do not be unwise, but understand what the will of the Lord is" (Eph. 5:15-17). We should be living in a wise and worthy manner, which means following the plan for which God gave us life. To truly accomplish this we must be guided daily by the Holy Spirit. When we live in such a way, we will find our lives are the most fulfilled.

Now is the time for the history makers to emerge and take their place. The Spirit of Truth is erasing a huge lie that has paralyzed the Body of Christ, which says God only uses the "superstar saint." Nothing could be farther from biblical truth. God uses ordinary people to accomplish extraordinary exploits. Remember, the promise of Isaiah 40:31 is for all who hope in the Lord: "But those who hope in the Lord will renew their strength. They will soar on wings like eagles; they will run and not grow weary, they will walk and not be faint" (NIV).

THE PREPARATION OF FRIENDSHIP

The Spirit of God has chosen you to live during these important days in history. Each of us should strive to accomplish great things for the glory of God. The greatest achievement we are called to is a continuing companionship and friendship with Christ. As we walk in this, we will become overcomers.

Our friendship with Christ helps prepare us for the harvest. The Church must be equipped to handle the coming waves of people. The masses of people that are coming will be from every walk and every level of society. Nothing can qualify us for this gathering of the harvest more quickly than friendship with Christ. It is only as the world takes notice that we have been with Christ that our witness will ring true.

This is what the leaders in Jerusalem said about Peter and John. "When they saw the courage of Peter and John, and realized that they were unschooled, ordinary men, they were astonished and they took note that these men had been with Jesus" (Acts 4:13). May the same be said about us; may the world see us as those who not only know *about* Christ, but *know* Him and are known *by* Him.

I have experienced the outstanding privilege of being in ministry meetings when suddenly the entire room is filled with the overwhelming smell of fresh baked bread. In most cases when this occurs we experience marvelous manifestations of divine healing. Jesus states that healing is the children's bread (see Mark 7:27). This bread for the sick and hurting is the Lord Jesus serving the bread of His presence, for He is the Healer. The Holy Spirit is releasing an awesome anointing for healing in our day; this anointing is going to be placed upon the Body of Christ.

In a prophetic visitation the Lord said to me, *"Tell the Church, ready or not here I come, and I have a gift in My hand...it is the gift of healing...it will be placed upon the Body not just upon somebody."* We have witnessed the marvelous gift of healing move and minister while resting upon somebody. For example Benny Hinn moves in an awesome gift of healing and miracles. This is wonderful, and we so appreciate all God is doing through this wonderful man of God; however what is coming will be far more awesome—a powerful anointing of healing and mighty miracles moving upon the entire Body of believers.

Many years ago, I was sent by the Lord to prophesy to Benny Hinn, telling him that soon there would come a day when children would be moving in the power and anointing he is walking in. I will never forget his response. His eyes danced and sparkled as he said with absolute joy, *"Bobby, I know, the Lord has also told me that!"* Let us pray for that day to fall upon us now.

We stand on the very verge of the largest healing movement in the history of the Church. One of the reasons this healing anointing is coming is that we are going to need it. It is time to pray for Heaven's bread to be served in our meetings, offering prayer for the sick, anointing with oil, praying the prayer of faith, and expecting the Lord to manifest Himself as the Bread of Heaven given for our healing.

BREAD FOR THE SINFUL AND HUNGRY

In Exodus 16, God answered the cry of His people for bread as they journeyed in the wilderness. This pure, white, round bread that God caused to rain down from Heaven upon His hungry people as they griped and grumbled about their wilderness walk, was a foreshadow or reflection of Christ Jesus. For example, sustenance came down from God out of Heaven; it was white, which speaks of purity; it was round, speaking of being endless, eternal. Christ declares that He is indeed the Bread sent down from Heaven. "I am the bread of life. He who comes to Me shall never hunger, and he who believes in Me shall never thirst" (John 6:35). How grateful we are to God for His wonderful provision of the Bread of Heaven. *Only as we receive and partake of Him do we have true life.* None need to starve or stumble in darkness, since we have been given the Light of the World and the true Bread of Life for our wilderness journey.

SHARING HEAVEN'S BREAD

It is time also to share the Bread of Heaven with hungry, hurting humanity. Our world is starving and desperate for Heaven's Bread—the Living Christ. There is a remarkable story recorded in the seventh chapter of Second Kings. Here we see people in the midst of a great famine. Never had there been such a desperate time. People were even stooping to cannibalism, eating their own children (see 2 Kings 6:25-29).

In the midst of such need, the prophetic word recorded in Second Kings 7:1 came to God's people. The prophet Elisha stood and declared boldly! "Hear the word of the Lord. Thus says the Lord, 'Tomorrow about this time a seah of fine flour shall be sold for a shekel, and two seahs of barley for a shekel, at the gate of Samaria.'" This is a bold prophetic statement. Right in the middle of this horrible famine, the prophet announces that on the next day there will be so much food available that it will almost be given away free.

We are instructed to trust in the Lord and we will be established, and to believe His prophets and we will prosper (see 2 Chron. 20:20). Notice the response of one of the not-so-wise leaders in Second Kings 7:2, who said in so many words that there is no way that even with God's intervention something like this could ever happen. To which Elisha replied, "...you will see it with your eyes, but you will not be one to take part in the provisions." You can see the outcome of this man's unbelief in Second Kings 7:17-19. He was trampled to death by the people rushing to eat of the food that God had provided. It is shocking and surprising how and who God used to provide such a mighty miracle. We must remember it is in our weakness that God's strength is made perfect, for when we are weak He is strong.

We must be like the four lepers in Second Kings 7:9. These pitiful, sick, dying men made a choice to change their situation. Asking the question, "Why sit here until we die?," they were compelled to get up and go forward, seeking a change. Can't you just see these four pitiful men with advanced leprosy as they stood upon their wounded feet that were infected and filled with painful sores? I can see them as they weakly stand, supporting each other as they attempt to steady their trembling bodies, limping off into the unknown, and knowing only that there must be more than what they are experiencing now.

What about you? Like the lepers, are you sick and tired of the lack of spiritual food? Are you ready to get up and advance into the unknown? Do you too need to ask yourself, "Am I going to sit here until I die?" We will never seek change if we are content with our situation.

As the lepers entered into the camp of the enemy soldiers who surrounded Jerusalem, they discovered it had been quickly and completely vacated. The enemy, in abject terror, had fled leaving behind not only the tables filled with wonderful bread and foods, but all their wealth. The question is how could four weak, pathetic lepers strike such terror and fear into the hearts of such a formidable foe? The answer is found in Second Kings 7:5-7. The Lord God had made the foe hear the sound of a mighty army advancing, bringing about these overwhelming results. When these four men entered the camp there was no opposition at all, only tables of food and tents filled with treasure. These starving men filled their stomachs full. Then they were filled with another hunger, the need to share what they had found with others. They were gripped with the understanding that they were responsible for sharing, with other starving people, the bread they had found.

For those of us to whom the Bread of Heaven has been given, we too must share Him with others. It is the cry of my heart that God will release outstanding grace for us to share Heaven's Bread with the hurting and hungry of the world. Amen!

My beloved spoke, and said to me: "Rise up, my love, my fair one, and come away" (Song of Solomon 2:10).

Jesus Christ said "Follow Me, and I will make you...." The Lord Jesus is beckoning us as His beloved Bride to fully follow *Him*. The invitation is extended—it is now time to respond. It is time to lay down our plans and follow the Lord. Jesus states in Matthew 16:24-25, "If any man will come after Me, let him deny himself, and take up his cross, and *follow Me*. For whosoever will save his life shall lose it: and whosoever will lose his life for My sake shall find it" (KJV). Again in John 12:26 we hear Jesus informing His disciples, "If any man serve Me, let him *follow Me*; and where I am, there shall also My servant be: if any man serve Me, him will My Father honor" (KJV).

During these days of preparation, nothing is more crucial than being with Jesus, and His presence being with you. This was Moses' desperate cry to God: that His presence would be with His people. "...If Your Presence does not go with us, do not bring us up from here. For how then will it be known that Your people and I have found grace in Your sight, except You go with us?" (Exod. 33:15-16). God delights in those who desire Him. It is those who seek after Him whom He chooses as His disciples.

It is easy to understand why God chose Joshua to be the leader after the death of Moses. The key is found in Exodus 33:11, "So the Lord spoke to Moses face to face, as a man speaks to his friend. And he would return to the camp, but his servant Joshua the son of Nun, a young man, did not depart from the tabernacle." Joshua loved being in the presence of God. Those who pursue the presence of God will find themselves following Christ and being formed into His disciples.

THE DEFINITION OF A DISCIPLE

Jesus' call to His disciples was to follow Him. But what exactly is a disciple? The New Testament word for "disciple" is the Greek word *mathetes*, which means "a learner." It comes from the root word *manthano*, which means "to learn." This word deals with *doing*, not just hearing. Being a disciple denotes having a belief that is accompanied by behavior. What we have learned is to change our attitude, which in turn changes our actions. You can say you believe something, but until what you believe changes your actions, you are just living in deception. So the word *disciple* denotes, "one who actively follows one's teaching." The "disciples" of Jesus.

A disciple is not only a *student*, but a *follower*; hence we are spoken of as imitators of our Teacher. Too many would-be disciples in our day are looking to classes instead of picking up their crosses. If we are students without becoming followers, we are in danger of becoming dead in spirit and bound in legalism. On the other hand, if we are followers without becoming true students, we are in danger of becoming superficial, shallow, cotton-candy Christians who cannot effect our world for Christ.

A total commitment is crucial if we are to fulfill the Great Commission. We are about to find out that well *done* is better than well *said*. It was never the plan of God to establish the Kingdom of God just by talking. It is going to take doing. "For the kingdom of God is not a matter of talk but of power" (1 Cor. 4:20 NIV). The revival came in Samaria when the people heard *and saw* the miracles Philip was doing. "And the multitudes with one accord heeded the things spoken by Philip, hearing and seeing the miracles which he did" (Acts 8:6). Notice the first verse of the Book of Acts, "The former account I made…of all that Jesus began both to *do* and *teach*." It is important to note that the Scriptures record what Jesus taught and did. We must be doers of the Word, and not just hearers of the Word. Otherwise we deceive ourselves. "But be doers of the word, and not hearers only, deceiving yourselves" (James 1:22).

CARPE DIEM—SEIZE THE DAY

It has been said, "We cannot direct the wind; however, we can adjust the sails," and the time has come for the Church to turn her sail to catch the wind of discipleship. We do not have time to waste; the only preparation for tomorrow is the right use of today. The Scriptures declare "…Behold, now is the accepted time…" (2 Cor. 6:2). It is time for the leaders in the Church to stop arguing about what a Christian is...and become one—a believing, following disciple of Christ! "...Be an example to the believers in word, in conduct, in love, in spirit, in faith, in purity" (1 Tim. 4:12). The coming leadership will be ordinary people with extraordinary determination—determination first and foremost to follow Jesus!

We have an open door to reach out with the gospel to hurting humanity. It is time we become disciples of Christ and not settle for being only believers in Him. We must stop fussing over what we don't agree on—and start sharing the good news of the gospel. Apostle Paul spoke about the importance of good doctrine, but he also said that if on some points you disagree, don't become divided. Instead, he exhorted us to keep walking out what we know while allowing God to make clear any apparent contradictions. "...And if on some point you think differently, that too God will make clear to you. Only let us live up to what we have already attained" (Phil. 3:15-16 NIV).

MARKS OF A DISCIPLE

There is no need to wonder if we are disciples of Christ or not. Jesus clearly defined what His disciples would look like. First, He said, "If you abide in My word, you are My disciples indeed" (John 8:31). When we abide in Christ's word, we confirm that we are one of His disciples. We must be like trees planted by the deep rivers of God's Word to bring forth fruit that will remain.

Jesus also said that His disciples will be doers. Their understanding will bring action. They will be like a prized apple tree in September—bearing much fruit for the Kingdom. "By this My Father is glorified, that you bear much fruit; so you will be My disciples" (John 15:8). Remember, Jesus is looking for doers; those who will be fruit-filled and fruitful.

The greatest proof of our discipleship, however, will not be our dogmatic adherence to doctrine, or the great things we accomplish in the name of Jesus, but rather it will be our love one for another.

"By this all will know that you are My disciples, if you have love for one another" (John 13:35). Let us choose to abide in His Word, press on to fruitfulness, and walk in His love so that we may truly be His disciples.

May God grant to each of us the grace to fully follow *Him* so that He can mold and make our lives into His image. "For whom He foreknew, He also predestined to be conformed to the image of His Son, that He might be the firstborn among many brethren" (Rom. 8:29).

Chapter 6

EVANGELISM IN THE NEW MILLENNIUM

⧄⧉⧄

DOUG ADDISON

Doug Addison is the founder of InLight Connection and is the author of *Prophecy, Dreams, and Evangelism* and his latest project, *Accelerating Into Your Life's Purpose*. He travels worldwide helping people transform their lives and discover their purpose. Doug is a stand-up comedian and his training seminars include hearing God, understanding dreams and visions, and experiencing the supernatural. Doug also trains and leads dream teams and prophetic/power evangelism outreaches. His Website is: www.dougaddison.com.

In this chapter Doug discusses the effects of evangelism in the new millennium.

A NEW SPIRITUAL HUNGER

It is not too difficult to notice a new spiritual hunger in people. The media are overflowing with television shows and movies related to spirituality. Shows like, *Charmed*, *Medium*, and *Buffy the Vampire Slayer* are indicators of the new openness people have to spirituality though these shows are not a positive influence. Psychics and palm readers that once only operated in carnival sideshows now have their own television shows, plush offices, and kiosks in malls. With this increasing interest in the occult and spirituality, one can not help but wonder if dark spiritual forces have invaded our society. I believe that we are seeing this spiritual renaissance because God Himself is planting a spiritual hunger in people and they are searching for understanding and fulfillment.

I've read that about 84 percent of Americans are longing for a deeper spiritual experience. People are responding to this spiritual awakening the only way they know how. Since many of these seekers have been wounded by a church or religious experience, they are often drawn to the New Age Movement and the occult, though their spiritual hunger will never truly be fulfilled through those venues.

In Acts 2:17-18, God says that in the last days He is going to pour out His Spirit on everyone and they will prophesy, see visions, and have dreams. As the Holy Spirit touches people they suddenly become aware of their emptiness, need for purpose, and direction in life.

We are now seeing millions of people who are open to spirituality. Unfortunately, most of our traditional evangelistic methods are not working as effectively as they once did. Acts 2:17-18 indicates that ministry in the last days will involve prophecy, dreams, and visions. People are being drawn to the supernatural and as Christians we need only to ask God to point them out to us. As we begin to hear God's plan for others, we can get ready for many divine encounters designed to bring people to Jesus Christ.

I have spent the past ten years doing prophetic and power evangelism outreaches in coffee houses, malls, and at New Age events and festivals. We are finding that people everywhere are very open to talking more about God right after we interpret their dream or give them a prophetic word from God through the Holy Spirit.

Unfortunately, many Christians are carrying evangelistic baggage from the past that prevents them from being relevant to the spiritual seekers of the new millennium. We were trained that unless we "close the deal" or turn every conversation to Jesus, we are compromising the gospel. We pretty much have used one approach to get people to come to Jesus by means of the Sinner's Prayer. Yet a closer look at how Jesus interacted with nonbelievers reveals that He customized each encounter to fit the person's needs.

Our society is rapidly changing and people are becoming immune to our evangelistic approaches. A popular quote from Jesus that is used often in evangelism is John 14:6, "Jesus said to him, 'I am the way, the truth, and the life. No one comes to the Father except through Me." People today are now turning this verse around and using it on us. They ask, "Do you believe that Jesus is the only way?" Our answer in the affirmative will cause a wall to go up and they usually are not interested in what else we have to say.

If you look at the context of this verse (and many of the other verses we currently use for evangelism), you will find that Jesus never spoke this way to an *unbeliever*. He said this to Thomas and the disciples long after they had chosen to follow Him. John 14:6 is not a good conversational ice breaker. I like to think of this verse as a three-step process necessary to bring someone to Christ. Show them the way; they discover the truth; and new life will be theirs.

Most people that we encounter are not as interested in truth as they once were, so we need to focus more on "showing people the way." Quoting Bible verses to people who don't believe in the validity of the Bible may not get the same result as it once did. This is because we are now dealing with a large number of people who no longer have a memory of Christianity in their life. The popular evangelistic methods of the past worked well—and still work well—with people who have some prior positive connection with Christianity.

We need a paradigm shift if we want to continue to reach people for Jesus. I would like to share a few things that I have found helpful in making this shift into what we consider to be a culturally relevant way to reach people with God's love.

OPENING PEOPLE'S EYES

In Acts 26:17-18 Saul (later named Paul) encounters Jesus on the road to Damascus. Jesus said, "I am sending you to the Gentiles to open their eyes, so they may turn from darkness to light and from the power of Satan to God. Then they will receive forgiveness for their sins..." (NLT).

Most evangelistic methods focus on turning people from darkness to light. Jesus, however, tells Saul to first open a person's eyes spiritually for them to turn from darkness. This involves demonstrating God's love and power to them (see 1 Cor. 2:4).

Let's do a quick study of the first seven chapters of the Gospel of John that gives an overview of how Jesus interacted with people. Note that He used the spiritual gifts, including words of knowledge, prophecy, and miracles, first to open people's eyes. Opening someone's eyes is very similar to showing them the way.

JESUS ENCOUNTERS NATHANAEL (JOHN 1:45-51)

Jesus drew Nathanael to follow Him by giving him a word of knowledge when He stated, "Here is a true Israelite, in whom there is nothing false." It must have been accurate because Nathanael was amazed that Jesus knew him. Jesus also told Nathanael that earlier

He had "seen" Nathanael sitting under a fig tree; perhaps it was where Nathanael had his prayer times with God, a place he could retreat to and let his hair down—for didn't Jesus call Nathanael a man of truth? Jesus went on to give him a word of prophecy for the future. This encounter opened Nathanael's eyes and caused him to declare, "Rabbi, You are the son of God, the King of Israel," and to become one of His followers.

JESUS ENCOUNTERS PEOPLE AT A WEDDING RECEPTION (JOHN 2:1-11)

This was Jesus' first recorded miracle, and what an astounding and symbolic one at that! Jesus knew the people needed a savior, but He also knew they had not had enough time with Him to understand the details of this. Jesus met the people's needs by providing wine, which also gained His disciples' attention because when they saw the miracle, they put their faith in Him. This miracle would make a great outreach!

JESUS ENCOUNTERS NICODEMUS, A RELIGIOUS LEADER (JOHN 3:1-21)

This is a powerful example of our need to be missionaries and learn to communicate with people in their "language." Jesus demonstrates this in His encounter with Nicodemus, a rabbi and teacher of Jewish law.

Nicodemus came secretly to Jesus seeking more information about His message. At first glance it's easy to miss the depth of Jesus' response to Nicodemus. In "missionary terminology," Jesus zeroed in on an aspect of Nicodemus' belief system by which He could relate His message: the Jewish culture and mindset of that time. Unlike the Western way of thinking, Jews viewed life on earth as a gestation period or prenatal experience in a womb, before birth into the true life of Paradise or Heaven. Life for a Jew encompassed the eternal reality of the spiritual world.

In the Western world, life is considered as space and time on earth, and Heaven is at a time in the future (derived from the Talmud[1]). Through the lens of the more holistic Jewish mindset, we can more fully appreciate the brilliance of John 3:3 when Jesus said, "Most assuredly, I say to you, unless one is born again, he cannot see the kingdom of God." Jesus went on to reveal more to Nicodemus, although at the time Nicodemus had trouble believing (see John 3:12).

The encounter with Nicodemus is one of the few in Scripture when Jesus sat and reasoned with someone without demonstrating God's power. Jesus knew that Nicodemus was an intelligent man versed in the Old Testament writings, so Jesus did not take the approach of refuting and quoting Scriptures to him. Instead, He translated His message into Nicodemus' cultural understanding and hinted that the signs concerning Himself were the fulfillment of biblical prophecies.

It obviously worked because Nicodemus later became a believer, standing up for Jesus during a meeting (see John 7:50) and helping to bury Jesus' body after His crucifixion (see John 19:39).

JESUS ENCOUNTERS THE SAMARITAN WOMAN (JOHN 4:7-30, 39-41)

Interestingly, in this encounter the Samaritan woman was aware that Rachel met Jacob, the man who changed her life, at a well (see Gen. 29:10). Yet, little did she know that she was about to meet a man at Jacob's Well who would also change her life. During their conversation, Jesus told the Samaritan woman a little about herself: she had been married five times and was not married to the man she now lived with. He did this without condemning her; He did it by a word of knowledge. Had Jesus been judging her, He would have called her an adulterous woman. Instead, He said to her, "What you said is quite honest." Jesus seemed to find the positive in people. As a result, the woman's response was "Sir, I perceive you to be a prophet." Nowadays, most people's response to this kind of clear insight would be, "Are you a psychic?"

Jesus had appraised her accurately: she was a relational nightmare. His compassion and concern for her, however, seemed to cut through her doubts, igniting such an evangelistic flame in her that she ran back to the town to tell everyone about Him, which caused many Samaritans to seek Jesus that day. Later, those who before this encounter would probably not have interacted with her at all told her, "We no longer believe just because of what you said; now we have heard for ourselves, and we know that this man really is the Savior of the world" (John 4:42 NIV). They, too, had had their eyes opened, and God turned them from darkness to light.

JESUS ENCOUNTERS A ROMAN OFFICIAL
(JOHN 4:46-52)

Jesus left Samaria and healed the son of a Roman noble without even meeting the child or laying hands on him. This miracle transcended distance, and the father realized his son had been healed at the exact moment Jesus declared, "Your son will live." So the Roman noble and his entire household believed in Jesus (see John 4:53).

JESUS ENCOUNTERS A PARALYZED MAN
(JOHN 5:1-9)

Jesus healed a man who had been paralyzed for 38 years. Not only was the man healed but he also required no rehabilitation, even after not using his legs for decades. After performing the miracle Jesus gave him further spiritual counsel:

"Later Jesus found him at the temple and said to him, 'See, you are well again. Stop sinning or something worse may happen to you.'

The man went away and told the Jews that it was Jesus who had made him well" (John 5:14-15 NIV). Notice that Jesus demonstrated God's healing power and got the man's attention before confronting him about his sin issues.

JESUS ENCOUNTERS 5,000 HUNGRY PEOPLE (JOHN 6:1-13)

Jesus and the disciples fed 5,000 people miraculously by multiplying five loaves of bread and two small fish. This was an eye-opening extravaganza! It must have worked because John 6:14 records: *"After the people saw the miraculous sign that Jesus did, they began to say, 'Surely this is the Prophet who is to come into the world.'"*

JESUS ENCOUNTERS HIS DISCIPLES ON THE WATER (JOHN 6:16-21)

Jesus walked on the water and caught up with His disciples in the middle of the Sea of Galilee. It's easy to miss—amid details as to how far Jesus' disciples had rowed before they saw Him walking on the water—just how significant this encounter with Jesus really is. When Jesus got in the boat, the Spirit immediately and miraculously transported Him, the boat, and His twelve disciples to the other side of the Sea of Galilee. This was so amazing that it caused an immediate increase in the disciples' faith.

Similar to this encounter was what happened to Philip after he baptized the Ethiopian eunuch. The Spirit of the Lord took him away, and he appeared at the town of Azotus (see Acts 8:39-40).

JESUS OPENED PEOPLE'S EYES TO GOD

Throughout the first six chapters of the Book of John, Jesus employed various means to "open people's eyes" before preaching to them. He demonstrated God's love and power in practical ways, with each encounter tailor-made to touch the particular individual or group He was addressing. Jesus used the spiritual gifts of words of knowledge, wisdom, prophecy, healing, and miracles. Yet He did not neglect to respond to their material, physical, and emotional needs as well—feeding the hungry, loving the outcasts, and bringing truth even when it caused Him to be hated. In short, whatever would get people to recognize the power and love of God, He did. As a result, people were looking for Him at the Feast of Tabernacles:

> *Now at the Feast the Jews were watching for him and asking, "Where is that man?"* (John 7:11 NIV)

UNDERSTANDING PEOPLE'S PROCESS

Another key to sharing God's love is to understand that people tend to realize their need for God through a process of circumstances and events in their lives. Jesus gives us insight into this process in Mark 4:26-29 (NIV):

> *He [Jesus] also said, "This is what the kingdom of God is like. A man scatters seed on the ground. Night and day, whether he sleeps or gets up, the seed sprouts and grows, though he does not know how. All by itself the soil produces grain—first the stalk, then the head, then the full kernel in the head. As soon as the grain is ripe, he puts the sickle to it, because the harvest has come."*

This parable clearly shows the process that seed goes through in order to grow. We must be careful not to be too eager or forceful in trying to get someone to pray a prayer of salvation, especially if they are not ready. Nowadays, people value friendships and like to consider themselves on their own journeys. In other words, they like to be given time to think about things and make their own choices.

Christians need to develop the art of discerning where people are in their journey to Jesus. Then we can work hand in hand with the Holy Spirit and be part of nudging them closer to God in a natural process.

SPEAKING RELEVANTLY WITH PEOPLE

One of the hardest things about trying to reach people is learning to communicate in a way that is understood by those without a religious background. Many Christians have developed an insider language that people outside the Church may not understand. We could easily pick some of these words up from reading the Bible. Here's a few examples: "like unto," "likened to," "whereby," "saith the Lord," or "thee," "thou," and "ye," and all the "iths," "eths," and "ests" added as suffixes. "I admonish thee: It behoovest ye ill to utter thusly whilst thou sojournest at the coffeepot at work!"

Too often the biggest barrier in sharing God's love is our own communication style. Apostle Paul addresses this in Colossians 4:4-6 (NIV):

> *Pray that I may proclaim it clearly, as I should. Be wise in the way you act toward outsiders; make the most of every opportunity. Let your conversation be always full of grace, seasoned with salt, so that you may know how to answer everyone.*

Paul encourages us to be clear in the way we speak and interact with those outside the Church. People are more likely to let down their walls of defense and talk openly when we are careful not to use religious words or Bible references that they might not understand.

At our outreach events we are finding that when we use a

non-religious style of communicating, people open up and talk more. They often say, "You sound different than most Christians. You actually seem normal."

LOVING AND ENCOURAGING PEOPLE

Another important factor in being culturally relevant with the message of Jesus is that you must be motivated by love. People can detect when you have an agenda to try to convert them and they will resist you. But when you truly care for them they will be drawn to the Spirit of love within you. I regard every encounter as being necessary and divinely orchestrated whether a person comes to know Jesus or not. I have given a person a word of encouragement to not give up or that God loves them and at the time it did not seem all that powerful. Later I found that it was the turning point of God revealing Himself to them.

In today's pop culture, "Reality TV" shows are popping up everywhere. These shows try to make rejecting people funny by using sayings like, "You're fired," "You're off the island," "You are voted out...." In reality, being mean and getting revenge is not how people really want to be treated. The "Makeover" shows on the other hand, tend to build people up. We need to consider ourselves as being part of "Extreme Makeover—God Edition."

It is evident with the increased popularity of psychics that people are longing to hear from God. When we act as God's messengers we must do so in a positive way. Guilt-based evangelism is not effective in a culture that goes to therapy to get rid of guilt. People today are gripped by fear, beat down, and stressed out. They long for encouragement and hope. According to First Corinthians 14:3, prophecy (or any form of revelation) is for strengthening, encouragement, and comfort, especially when it is used as a means of evangelism. Pointing out a person's sin or being confrontational in a rude way is not an encouraging or effective way to draw them to God.

IN SUMMARY

As we think about evangelism in the new millennium, we need to view ourselves as missionaries in our own communities.

As we change our approach to be more culturally relevant, God will use us to draw people to Jesus Christ. Try replacing the "Free Prayer" sign on the booth at a fair with "Free Encouragement." Help people understand their dreams by viewing them similarly to a parable. Offer seminars on finding your destiny but don't do a "bait-n-switch" and turn it into an altar call. Find creative ways to connect with people and get to know them first.

I found it interesting that Starbucks Coffee was able to influence the world in a positive way for coffee without ever trying to convince people that they "need coffee." Instead, they tapped into what people value today: community and an environment for self-discovery. I am convinced that we need more Christian bookstores that allow people to hang out, read books, drink coffee, and enjoy.

We can be naturally supernatural and find that evangelism is actually fun, easy to do, and much more accepted by those around us. The sky is the limit. We don't want to change the message of Jesus... but we can change the way we share it!

ENDNOTE

1. The Shéma Yisrael Torah Network: Before life on earth begins, a person exists in his or her mother's womb and it is the source of sustenance. At birth, a person leaves the womb of his or her mother and enters the womb of earth. Earth is like the mother's womb because during a person's lifetime, it is the source of sustenance. Similarly, at death, a person leaves the womb of earth and enters the womb of creation. Accessed at: http://www.shemayisrael.co.il/burial/bur1.htm.

Chapter 7

TESTIMONIES OF THE SUPERNATURAL OPENS DOORS TO SHARE THE GOSPEL

DAVID TOMBERLIN

While attending college, David had a dramatic encounter with the Holy Spirit that forever changed his life. Since that time, the Lord has used David to lead many to Christ. By God's grace, he has traveled to more than 30 countries and ministers the Word of God with miracles, signs and wonders following. David's heart's desire is to see true revival in the church, and for the lost to come to Christ.

David shares his testimony with you:

THE WORD OF OUR TESTIMONY

There I was in a rural mountain village in Japan. I had just finished snowboarding with American and Canadian friends that I had made the previous year while living and working a secular job in Japan. The people I was with had always been very friendly, we always got along and had a good time. At some level, though, I think they didn't know quite how to take me. On the one hand, I was a fun-loving, energetic, friendly guy who had a lot of friends and seemed pretty "normal." But on the other hand, I was a "Christian" who could often be found missing meals (fasting) or driving 90 minutes one way to go to church every Sunday. Although I was average and even fun, it was the whole "religious thing" that threw them off. They even seemed somewhat fearful of this side of me. They liked me but had a hard time knowing how to act around me.

After snowboarding that day, everyone was tired and we headed back to one of the guy's small Japanese apartment. Someone brought up my background as a "minister," and asked exactly how I got involved in that. I said that I had been studying business in college when I had a radical spiritual experience that changed my life. After that experience, I wanted to devote my life to serving God. Usually when I tell non-Christians that, I stop there, and depending on their interest level, I move forward. This time, someone asked me what kind of experience I had.

At that point I unleashed my full testimony—holding nothing back. "I had an experience that the Bible calls the Baptism of the Holy Spirit. This is when God puts His Spirit in you, to make you more like Christ." Then I told them all about how it went down.

"There I was in college. I had been given the MVP award on my college soccer team and a couple of professional teams talked to me about going pro. I owned two cars, I owned my own house (at age 21), and I had a beautiful girlfriend. Even with all of these external things going so well, for some unknown reason, I went into a horrible depression. I began to get cold shivers and hot sweats when I slept. I would close my eyes and see demons, and even at times I would feel as though I was coming out of my body. The torment was so bad that I planned a couple of times to kill myself.

"I also had this terrible choking feeling around my neck all the time, the only time it would leave is when I would go to church. So I started going to church more.

"One night while at church, a man of God named Sam Farina was preaching on the Baptism of the Holy Spirit with the evidence of speaking in tongues. I didn't know what to think about this because my conservative friends said that this baptism was fake. I always considered myself a genuine person and loathed anything fake, so I told the Lord, 'God, I want anything you have for me, but I am not faking anything.'

"As Brother Farina was praying for people, I closed my eyes and saw a golden light. I really had no idea what was going on. Then as he laid hands on me, tongues started shooting out of my mouth. It wasn't like I was trying, it was more like I was watching it happen, but still thinking of my friend who told me it was fake. I thought to myself, *I wonder if I am faking this?* Just as the thought came to my mind Sam yelled, 'YOU'RE NOT FAKING THIS!'

"The next thing I remember I was lying on my back. I felt like something was swirling in my stomach and I saw three evil spirits leave my body. I felt clean and pure and more alive than I ever had in my entire life. A voice spoke to me and said 'This is what Heaven is like.' Ever since that day I felt called into the ministry."

A silence was in the room and my friends started asking me questions, "Why do you think God picked you?" I told them that this was not as rare as they might think; 700 million people in the world who are Pentecostal or Charismatics—one out of about ten people on the planet— have experienced the same thing. I said this gift is available to all those who follow Jesus, and shared the entire gospel with them. They were so open!

In that group there was a Muslim, Buddhist, Jew, and two people with Christian backgrounds who were not following the Lord. A holy reverence for the Lord was there that night as we talked for quite a while about the things of God. In each of them was planted a gospel seed, not because it was forced down their throat, but because they were hungry for the supernatural and were eager to hear all about the supernatural God I serve.

Once I was spending the day with a medical doctor friend of mine. He had brought with him another doctor, a Russian Jew who was not a follower of Jesus but was an influential leader in the medical community. In sharing his credentials, he let me know that he was not only a medical doctor, but had spent time as a professor at the flagship medical research school and hospital, Johns Hopkins. He was a kind man, and took great interest in the fact that I was a minister. My doctor friend had introduced me as "a very spiritual man who has had a lot of experience with God." As the day went by I shared my personal testimony about how I was baptized in the Holy Spirit as well as other healing and deliverance testimonies. He was amazed, and by the end of the evening he bowed his head and I had the privilege of praying the sinner's prayer with him.

TESTIMONIES OF THE SUPERNATURAL

John 9:25: *"He replied, 'Whether he is a sinner or not, I don't know. One thing I do know. I was blind but now I see!'"*

Often at our David Tomberlin Ministries' conferences we have what we call Vision and Impartation luncheons. It's a time to get to know people in a more relaxed setting, and we share more about our ministry's vision. At the conclusion we have a time of prayer and impartation. During one of our first luncheons, a young lady who came regularly to our meetings brought her unsaved husband. I didn't know he was unsaved so as I moved down the impartation line, expecting everyone to be saved.

As I laid hands on him, I prayed a general blessing and impartation over him and began to move to the next person but was drawn back to him by the Holy Spirit. I said, "I just saw a vision of snakes coiled up attacking you. I break that curse over your life in Jesus' name!" Then I moved on to the next person.

After the luncheon the man's wife came up to me. "My husband doesn't know the Lord, and is freaked out by the word you gave him about the snakes." She said her husband was freaking because all that week he had been having nightmares of snakes coiled up striking at him. Because of that word, he gave his life to the Lord and shortly thereafter I had the privilege of baptizing him in water. He serves the Lord to this day because of the testimony of the supernatural that he experienced that brought him to the Lord.

SIGNS TO UNBELIEVERS

Not long ago I was a guest on the TBN *Praise the Lord* television program. My family was excited for me and watched it along with their extended family, friends, and neighbors. (I think the ratings went up significantly from my family and friends watching.) During the program the Lord was gracious to me, and I called out several words of knowledge and prophesied over one young woman who wept as I gave her the word she later confirmed. I also called out people with back problems and two or three men were healed on the spot as I prayed for their legs to grow. Because one leg was shorter than the other, it was causing their back problems. I also shared many testimonies of supernatural healings and angelic encounters on the program. The presence of God was there, and I had a nice time in Dallas with host Richard Hogue and singing guest J. Moss.

After the program, one of my brothers told me about his brother-in-law, who was not a believer. He watched the program and was glued to the screen, saying, "I love this stuff!" To my knowledge that was the first time he had ever witnessed the gospel message with any supernatural power behind it. He was deeply moved by the supernatural testimony of Jesus and received the seed of the gospel into his life.

As I flew home from the filming of the television program, I was sitting next to two women, probably in their early to mid-twenties. As we spoke, I found out that one of them lived just a few blocks from where I lived in Pasadena, California. They were in Dallas for a trade show, and the conversation moved to what I was doing there. I told them that I had just finished taping a Christian television program. They asked how it went, and I shared the supernatural testimonies of the evening.

"God was so good to us; He really blessed the people there. I prophesied over a lady there."

"What does that mean?" one asked.

"It means that God speaks to me something about them and I tell them what He said."

"You mean like fortune telling?"

"Yeah, something like that, but it comes from a different source, the Holy Spirit. We also prayed for some guys who had back pain and we found that their one leg was shorter than the other, so as I prayed, their legs grew longer. It was awesome!"

"How did you get involved in all this?"

I then shared my testimony about how I received the Baptism of the Holy Spirit. The conversation flowed for what seemed like the entire flight back to Los Angeles. Before we parted they gave me their business cards and asked me to stay in touch with them. They wanted to come hear me speak and learn more about what I had shared with them.

In all of these examples I wasn't "trying to witness." I was just someone in a conversation with others. Through the natural course of our interaction, and the leading of the Holy Spirit, the subject comes up. Also, *they* were interested in the supernatural. *We call them "testimonies," but to unbelievers they are really awesome stories of stuff that they had never heard of before.*

Time after time, people's responses are, "Why does this happen to you," or "I would love to experience something like that," or "I didn't know Christianity could be like that." They are pleasantly surprised, instead of rudely interrupted with a forced "Gospel Presentation," which is often done in an unnatural, ham-fisted way.

TWOFOLD PROBLEM

I believe the problem with the way we have done evangelism in the past is twofold: (1) There is a misunderstanding of what the gospel is, and (2) we are motivated through guilt to preach the gospel and snatch people from the fiery furnace before judgment comes upon them instead of being motivated by the goodness of God.

I believe that in the past the church thought that the gospel was a series of doctrinal views that led to salvation. The checklist went something like this:

- Do you believe in the Virgin birth?
- Do you believe that Jesus lived a sinless life?
- Do you believe that Jesus died on the cross for your sins?
- Do you believe that Jesus rose again after three days and thereafter ascended into Heaven?
- Do you believe that if you confess your sins and ask Jesus for forgiveness you will be forgiven and go to Heaven instead of hell?

Yes? OK, you're a Christian.

For Jesus it was not a checklist of doctrines to mentally agree to, it was a question of did they believe "in" Him, and then if they really did, they would then follow Him. It was an issue of the heart and commitment being backed up by a lifestyle of following Him, doing the very things He did.

It was also an invitation within the context of a tangible manifestation of the very Kingdom that Jesus proclaimed. The problem with the way the gospel is presented today is that it makes great claims, but often lacks the power to back those claims. It is often said from the pulpit, "We serve the greatest God in *all the universe!*" "He is all powerful, all knowing." "In the Bible He performed great signs and miracles."

We carry on like this, but then there is no demonstration of this supposed power of God that we proclaim. Jesus never operated in such duplicity. He proclaimed the Kingdom and *demonstrated* the Kingdom. He said, "...if I cast out devils by the Spirit of God, surely the kingdom of God has come upon you (Matt. 12:28).

The use of supernatural testimonies is so powerful because it is not just a presentation of the gospel that gives doctrinal views, but it testifies to the real power of God that is truly imbedded in the gospel itself.

Peter used supernatural testimonies when he was describing Jesus' ministry to Cornelius, he said, "You know what has happened throughout Judea, beginning in Galilee after the baptism that John preached how God anointed Jesus of Nazareth with the Holy Spirit and power, and how He went around doing good and healing all who were under the power of the devil, because God was with Him" (Acts 10:37-38). The testimony of Jesus' life is so impacting because He did not just talk, He moved and demonstrated the supernatural reality that He proclaimed. Then after Peter shared the testimony— *he* moved in the power of God as well.

Integrity in the Kingdom of God is to witness and testify of a powerful God and then move in the power we proclaim— witnessing, preaching, and testifying without the power of God is duplicitous. We must walk in the power and testify to the power of God—miracles, signs and wonders, healing, prophecy, deliverance, visions, dreams, and angelic encounters should all be common for the believer. What we need is a transition from an intellectualized gospel, particularly here in the West, to a *supernatural gospel*, that displays the power it proclaims. This all begins by sharing supernatural testimonies. In fact the Scripture says, "...For the testimony of Jesus is the spirit of prophecy" (Rev. 19:10). Every true testimony of Jesus has prophetic anointing released with it.

SUPERNATURAL TESTIMONIES OPEN DOORS FOR BELIEVERS TO GROW

Acts 18:24-26 (NIV): "Meanwhile a Jew named Apollos, a native of Alexandria, came to Ephesus. He was a learned man, with a thorough knowledge of the Scriptures. He had been instructed in the way of the Lord, and he spoke with great fervor and taught about Jesus accurately, though *he knew only the baptism of John*. He began to speak boldly in the synagogue. When Priscilla and Aquila heard him, they invited him to their home and explained to him the way of God more adequately."

When this passage speaks of Apollos "knowing only the baptism of John" it is speaking of his being a Christian who is water baptized but has not yet received the Baptism of the Holy Spirit that Jesus talked about in Acts 1:4-5: Do not leave Jerusalem, but wait for the gift my Father promised, which you have heard me speak about. *"For John baptized with water, but in a few days you will be baptized with the Holy Spirit"* (NIV).

All of the people Jesus was speaking to loved Him, accepted Him, and followed Him; but they had not yet been empowered for service, through the Baptism of the Holy Spirit. The Baptism of the Holy Spirit is an empowering that enables us to be genuine witnesses of the power and goodness of God to the world.

Jesus said, regarding the Holy Spirit baptism, "...you will receive power when the Holy Spirit comes on you; and you will be my witnesses in Jerusalem, and in all Judea and Samaria, and to the ends of the earth" (Acts 1:8 NIV).

Less than a week before this writing I was ministering at a conference in Louisiana. It was an awesome gathering, the power of God was flowing, the prophetic was very strong and there were several wonderful healings under this anointing; several of those in a backslidden state rededicated themselves to the Lord. It was a powerful time in the Lord. One case really stood out:

There was a very nice man who was probably in his mid- to late sixties who came with his son-in-law and daughter. They had been inviting him for some time to attend the conference meetings, but after she would tell him about the supernatural power of God, he would say, "That's wonderful, but I don't think I will go." He finally relented and came to the meeting. Although he loved the Lord, his "conservative" denomination did not believe in the Baptism of the Holy Spirit, the gifts of the Spirit, or the general moving of the Spirit. He believed in reading and memorizing the Bible, but doing what was in the Bible was a different matter.

This man, like Apollos, had only known *the baptism of John,* he didn't know the Baptism of the Holy Spirit with the evidence of speaking in tongues or prophecy. Thankfully the conference host, Sharnael Wolverton, gave a spontaneous altar call for the Baptism of the Holy Spirit and to receive the accompanying gift of tongues as those in the upper room did in Acts.

The man came forward and after being prayed over, he was instantly baptized in the Holy Spirit and spoke in tongues. With hands lifted to the heavens he was gloriously baptized in the Holy Spirit and wept as the supernatural gift of tongues flowed from his innermost being. The glory of God shone on his face. The goodness of God was being poured out on his life and he was truly empowered to be a witness. He was changed forever, and received power to live the Christian life all because of the supernatural testimonies that his daughter and son-in-law consistently shared with him until he himself wanted to receive.

On another occasion I was in a Denny's restaurant in Pennsylvania during an internship program with my mentor and friend, where we were learning to grow in the supernatural. Several of us were eating dinner quite late one evening after a meeting, and we started challenging each other to get a word for our server. As we talked to him I saw the words "backslider" written in the spirit over his head. The letters formed an upside down "u" or an arch over and around his head. I thought, *How am I supposed to give this word?* We shared with him about what was going on in the meetings, and testified to the supernatural move of God we were seeing. He mentioned that he was going to two churches at the time and was involved in music in the church.

After he said that I asked, "How is your walk going with the Lord?" I asked in a tone that was suggesting there might be a problem. He looked at me right in the eye and said, "Not good... not good."

I said, "That makes sense because the Lord just showed me the word, *Backslider* written over your head. Today is a good day to get right with the Lord."

He gave me a somber smile.

As the evening went on we talked with him more and prayed with him and gave him a big tip to tangibly show our love and brotherhood with him.

As we left I knew that he was encouraged to get back with the Lord and delve into the supernatural reality of the Kingdom of God. He was really appreciative, and a weight seemed to be lifted off of his shoulders. What a relief it is for people when they know how real God is and how much He loves them despite their sin. As the Lord proves Himself through the supernatural testimony of Christ, lives are truly changed. Christians in sin or not filled with the Holy Spirit can receive the fullness of the King and His Kingdom and can be restored to right relationship with Him.

THE POWER OF THE TESTIMONY

The wonderful thing about using supernatural testimonies as a way to win souls or encourage believers is that it can be brought up in everyday conversation. Many times I have shared supernatural testimonies regarding a healing or miracle and people instantly ask me to pray for them and they receive the Lord or a healing.

There is something about remembering what the Father has done in the past that releases His glory in the present. Those very testimonies release the realm that brought the supernatural experience with the Lord in the first place. As Peter remembered what the Lord had done and shared the works of Christ to Cornelius' household, the Spirit of God fell and the people were baptized by the Spirit as he preached.

We are witnesses of everything He did in the country of the Jews and in Jerusalem. They killed Him by hanging Him on a tree, but God raised Him from the dead on the third day and caused Him to be seen. He was not seen by all the people, but by witnesses whom God had already chosen—by us who ate and drank with Him after He rose from the dead. He commanded us to preach to the people and to testify that He is the one whom God appointed as judge of the living and the dead. All the prophets testify about Him that everyone who believes in Him receives forgiveness of sins through His name.

While Peter was still speaking these words, the Holy Spirit came on all who heard the message. The circumcised believers who had come with Peter were astonished that the gift of the Holy Spirit had been poured out even on the Gentiles. For they heard them speaking in tongues and praising God (Acts 10:39-46 NIV).

The Holy Spirit came on the unbelievers as Peter was releasing the testimony. The power of God is literally embedded in the testimony and begins to work in the hearts and lives of people turning their hearts to God, creating a receptivity to the gospel message and the Baptism of the Holy Spirit.

FEED THE HUNGRY

I was ministering at a series of meetings in Canada when I met a young man. This young man had grown up as the child of a pastor in a conservative denomination. He had attended Sunday school, church every Sunday, vacation Bible school, youth group, and had grown up learning, reading, and memorizing Scripture. The only problem: there was no understanding of the Baptism of the Holy Spirit and the power of God. His denomination had taught that the gifts of the Holy Spirit had ceased after the first century, a heresy known as cessationism.

So when this young man had a back injury that put him out of work, the church he attended had no answers, except perhaps "God is trying to teach you something," or "This will help build your character." These religious people would have gotten along great with Job's counselors. Anyway, this young man heard that there were psychics who said they had the power to heal. He went to them and his back was healed. The young man was so excited that he became a psychic healer and led many people down the same path of destruction he was on.

After several years the Lord drew this young man back to Himself, back to a gospel with life, power, miracles, and healings. He rededicated his life to the Lord and ministry.

There is a hunger for the Lord in the earth today. The problem: many in the world associate the Lord with dry, crusty, legalistic, and often racist traditions that are dead, powerless expressions of religion, with no true knowledge of who God truly is. Unbelievers have no idea who the Lord is because many claiming to know and follow Him do not really know Him or His ways. The Church must be the answer for the spiritually hungry in the earth and we must embrace the supernatural God that we serve.

Release the supernatural testimonies of Heaven, and watch the world receive the Lord Jesus Christ!

Chapter 8

THE MISSING DIMENSION

⟨◊⟩

CHARLES H. KRAFT

Charles H. Kraft has been a member of the faculty of the School of World Mission (now School of Intercultural Studies) at Fuller Theological Seminary for 39 years. He serves as professor of Anthropology and Intercultural Communication, teaching anthropology, communication, contextualization, and spiritual dynamics (inner healing, deliverance, and spiritual warfare).

He holds degrees from Wheaton College (BA anthropology), Ashland Theological Seminary (BD theology), and Hartford Seminary Foundation (PhD anthropological linguistics). He served as a pioneer missionary among a tribal group (Kamwe) in northeastern Nigeria for three years followed by five years each on the faculties of Michigan State University and UCLA teaching linguistics and African languages. He is the author of 29 books and numerous articles in the fields of missiology, anthropology, communication, inner healing and deliverance, spiritual warfare, and African languages and linguistics.

Dr. Kraft is also an ordained minister, and he shares his years of experience with the Lord with you:

JESUS' LOVE RELATIONSHIP

In my 2002 book *Confronting Powerless Christianity¹*, I have suggested that biblical Christianity can be viewed as made up of three distinct but complementary "crucial dimensions." These may be labeled:

1. Allegiance leading to Relationship;

2. Truth/Knowledge leading to Understanding; and

3. Spiritual Power leading to Freedom.

All aspects of biblical Christianity fit into these three categories; and if we are to practice a truly biblical and balanced Christianity, we need to give proper attention to the contents of each of these three dimensions.

A typical Jesus ministry event included all three. We find Him regularly teaching truth, interrupting His teaching to use spiritual power to heal or deliver someone, all the while appealing to His hearers to pledge allegiance to Him and to grow in their relationship with Him and the Christian family members.

Jesus' teaching was usually focused on relational subjects such as love, faith, forgiveness, repentance, reconciliation, and the like. And His teaching style was relational, spending night and day for three years with twelve disciples. Jesus' use of power, then, was intended to demonstrate God's love for hurting humans. His power is wrapped in a love relationship. Jesus' practice of a love relationship with humans and His teaching on relational topics make it clear that relationship is the most important of these three dimensions.

The picture I like to draw shows relationship (pictured as a table top) as primary with truth and spiritual power (pictured as the legs of the table), as supports for growth in our relationship with Him.

> *Relationship*
> *To God*
> *To others*
> *To self.*
> (see Matthew 22:37-40).

The two Great Commandments show that relationship is to be in the "number one" position: we are to love the Lord our God with all our heart, soul, and mind and our neighbors as ourselves (see Matt. 22:37-38). Love is the supreme expression of a proper relationship and a major theme of Scripture. Truth and knowledge on the one hand and spiritual power on the other are intended to support love, faith, repentance, forgiveness, and all the other aspects of our relationships with God and others.

INTENDED FUNCTIONS OF THE DIMENSIONS

All three of these dimensions are important for the proper understanding and experience of Christianity. Pledging allegiance to

Jesus Christ is essential if we are to call ourselves Christians. This allegiance is expected to issue in the growing of the relationship with Him that started at the point when we gave our lives to Him. This relationship is to be first in our lives with all other relationships secondary to it. We are to put Jesus first.

So as we grow closer and closer to Jesus, we are expected to experience growth in our relationship with Him and also in our relationship with others and with ourselves. The process of growth is, however, often impeded in evangelical circles by the fact that not enough attention is given to building the relationships as compared with the attention given to increasing cognitive knowledge (see below).

The intended function of the knowledge/truth dimension is to be a support of the relationship dimension. Knowing things about our faith is intended to lead us closer to Jesus, neighbors, and self. As with all knowledge, we should learn a little, then practice it, learn a little more, practice it, and so forth. Rather than simply accumulating information about the Christian life, we should be practicing in real life what we understand from Scripture and from the examples of our mentors with the aim of growing closer and closer to Jesus and more and more like Him in our behavior.

The purpose of the spiritual power dimension, then, is to free us from the things that bind us and hinder the process of growing closer to Jesus. Frequently people come to me for inner healing because they cannot get as close to Jesus as they want to. Invariably, it is because of deep-level hurts and habits that can only be healed through the power of Christ. When these people can experience the presence of Jesus in the damaging events of the past and give Him their hurts, they find themselves spiritually free and can get close to Him.

The purpose of using spiritual power to bring freedom is, therefore, to enable greater intimacy in our relationship with Jesus and our relationship with others as well. Both truth and knowledge leading to understanding and spiritual power leading to freedom are designed to result in greater growth in our relationship with Jesus.

THREE DIMENSIONS DEFINED

To clarify the three dimensions, the following charts outline the characteristics of each. First is the all-important Allegiance/Relationship Dimension:

THE ALLEGIANCE DIMENSION

Primary concern: *Relationship*

The most important of the three dimensions.

- Starts with conversion—a commitment to Christ—to establish a saving relationship with God through Jesus Christ.
- Aim is to replace any other allegiances/relationships as primary—all other allegiances are to be secondary to this one.
- It continues as growth in one's relationship with Christ and with others, expressed as loving God with one's whole heart and one's neighbor as oneself.
- It includes all that the Bible teaches on subjects like love, faith(fulness), fellowship, the fruits of the Spirit, intimacy with Christ (e.g., John 15), forgiveness, repentance, reconciliation, obedience.

- True intimacy and relationship should not be confused with *knowledge about* intimacy and relationship.
- All other allegiances are to be countered with commitment to Christ.
- Under this dimension, the church is to be experienced as *family.*
- Witness to one's personal experience is key to communicating this dimension.
- Theology is experienced in worship and submission to God (see Rom. 12:2).

The second dimension and the one most in focus in Evangelical circles is the Truth/Knowledge/Understanding Dimension:

THE TRUTH DIMENSION

Primary concern: *Understanding*

- This dimension involves teaching led by the Holy Spirit (see John 16:13).
- Scripturally, both truth and knowledge are experiential, not simply cognitive.
- Truth provides antidotes for ignorance and error.
- Though spiritual truth is pervasively relational and experiential (see John 8:32), there is also a cognitive and informational dimension.
- This dimension embodies truth and knowledge of all aspects of Christian experience.

- We are to learn in this dimension about the contents of the other two dimensions.
- We are expected to grow in this knowledge dimension as in all other dimensions of Christian experience.
- Satanic and human lies are to be countered with God's truths.
- Under this dimension, the church is to be experienced as a teaching place (discipleship, mentoring, classroom).
- Theology is both cognitive and experiential.

The third dimension, the one I'm calling, "The Missing Dimension," is the Spiritual Power/Freedom Dimension:

SPIRITUAL POWER DIMENSION

Primary concern: *Freedom*

- The power in focus here is spiritual power (not political, personal, etc.).
- This dimension recognizes that humans are held captive by satan.
- Jesus worked in the power of the Holy Spirit to set captives free (see Luke 4:18-19)—He did nothing under the power of His own divinity (see Phil. 2:5-8).
- Jesus passed this power on to His followers (see Luke 9:1; John 14:12; Acts 1:4-8).
- Satanic power must be defeated with God's power (it cannot be defeated simply with

truth or a correct allegiance, though these help).

- Under this dimension, the church is experienced as both a hospital where wounds are healed, thus freeing people, and an army that attacks the enemy, defeating him both at ground level and at cosmic level.
- Awareness of the spiritual power dimension of Christianity needs to be taught both cognitively and especially experientially (as Jesus did).
- Theology is experienced as victory in warfare resulting in freedom to relate and think.

THE PROBLEM

Even though there are three crucial dimensions, as evangelicals we have tended to put our primary focus on truth and knowledge, treating relationships as if they are automatically produced and nourished by an increase of knowledge and information. We specialize in the transmission of information in sermonizing, lecturing, and writing, assuming that what people need for growth is more information. In church and school our tendency is to *think about* things rather than to *do* them.

We do relate to God and others but it is truth and knowledge that are in focus in our teaching and the all-important relational aspects of our faith more talked about than practiced. So relationship is seen as simply a by-product of our thinking rather than the central focus it ought to be. This can be deadly as we see large numbers of students who go to Bible schools, Christian colleges, and seminaries sustaining spiritual damage because their faith is inundated with knowledge and their relationship with Jesus starved.

Though neglected, the relationship part of our faith does receive some attention from evangelicals. We all hold that a person must be born again into a relationship with God through Jesus. We speak of salvation through faith in Christ as a distinctive of evangelical doctrine and life. Evangelicals would even admit that our relationship with God is more important than our knowledge about Him.

Unfortunately, however, many don't go much further than this initial acceptance of Jesus in their relationship with Him. He is Savior but often not Lord. And if we go to Bible school or seminary, the focus is usually so much on knowledge and information that many find their relationship with God moved to a "back burner" and suffering neglect.

As a young Christian I was taught to witness to others largely by feeding them information about Christ and then inviting them to accept Jesus as their personal Savior. When that pattern is followed, though, we are asking a person to jump from the truth/knowledge/understanding dimension to the allegiance/relationship dimension. When truth/knowledge is in focus, the expected aim is understanding. If we want people to come to allegiance, though, we need to witness concerning experience, not simply add to a person's knowledge because these two are on completely different dimensions of life and behavior.

When the lead-up is increase of knowledge, there is no bridge to the experiential commitment to Christ. In order to get there, a person has to make a "leap" from the knowledge dimension he/she has been focused on to the allegiance dimension in which saving faith is experienced. Recognizing that we have to switch dimensions to arrive at faith shows up the fault of many evangelicals who downplay experience in favor of knowledge, thus damaging the all-important need for growth in relationship.

STRONG ON KNOWLEDGE, WEAK ON FAITH

Statements of faith are usually focused on cognitive expressions of belief, tending to ignore the growth in experience that is crucial to relational development. We thus produce many Christians strong on knowledge and belief but weak on faith and relationship.

But we have at least some emphasis on relationships to go along with our emphasis on truth. When it comes to the third of our dimensions, spiritual power, most evangelical churches and training institutions are guilty of total neglect, at least in practice. Though it is not uncommon to hear references to spiritual warfare in sermons and lectures, the references tend to be in the *knowledge about* category rather than in the *doing* category.

I regularly interact with pastors and sincere laypersons who know a bit about satanic activity but have no idea what to do to set captives free from it. So at the level of practice, this dimension of biblical Christianity is missing for them.

If Christianity is likened to a 300-piece picture puzzle, we Evangelicals have 100 of the pieces firmly in view (truth) with another 100 (relationship) out of focus but there to work with. It is the final 100 pieces that are the problem. This part of the puzzle is what I call "The Missing Dimension."

Yet Jesus said in Luke 10 that His disciples should communicate to the people of the villages to which He sent them that it was power demonstrations that signaled that the Kingdom had come near them (see Luke 10:9). It's when healings and deliverance from demons are practiced by Jesus and His followers that the Kingdom is demonstrated (see Matt 12:28; Luke 11:20).

I wonder if it is too much to conclude that if these power things are not happening, the Kingdom is not happening! In any event, the powerlessness of our Christianity contrasts markedly with the way Jesus presented His Kingdom. He came to a people who, like most of the world's peoples then and now, are looking for more spiritual power with a presentation of a God of love and power. We tend to go with a philosophical understanding and presentation of our faith with little or no demonstration of the power of Jesus.

WHY IS THIS DIMENSION MISSING?

I believe we have been seduced by the world and more specifically by the "academicization" of our faith to turn Christianity more into "a head thing" than it should be. Our so-called "worship services" are centered on intellectual presentations we call sermons, usually based on an information-oriented approach to biblical content. This is presented in lecture fashion to people who sit in rows like students or spectators.

Following Jesus' example, we have rightly focused on the teaching of truth. But we have reduced truth to a cognitive thing rather than an experiential thing. We often quote John 8:32: "You shall know the truth and the truth will set you free" (KJV). But we have missed the fact that both in the Hebrew thinking that lies behind the New Testament and even in the Greek, the kind of truth in view here is *experiential* truth, not cognitive truth. Jesus tells us that we are to gain freedom not by *thinking* truth but by *experiencing* it. A translation of that verse that would capture Jesus' intent would be: "You will *experience* the truth and the truth will set you free."

Perhaps our problem goes back to the Reformers or even to the Hellenizing of Christianity. The Reformers were academics. Their focus was on thinking right. The Greeks, of course, were fond of academic things as well. Debating was considered a sport, both outside and within the church. And within Christianity, those who the party in power felt were thinking wrongly were often persecuted harshly.

All this may have been complicated, then, by a focus on church rather than a focus on Kingdom. Jesus' focus was constantly on the Kingdom, a power concept. By comparison, the church is a much lesser theme in the New Testament. Though the New Testament is strong that believers should gather in groups called churches, it is the task of the churches to serve and establish the Kingdom.

HOW DO WE EXPERIENCE TRUTH?

I have suggested that we need to *experience* the truth rather than just *think* it or even to believe it. Jesus' ministry was one of works as well as words. In fact, He says to the doubters: If you don't believe my words, believe me because of the works I do (see John 10:38). Experiencing Jesus in words or works is experiencing truth. But it is experiencing the presence of Jesus, not simply listening to a lecture or participating in a discussion of truths about Him that is in view here.

An effective way to experience Jesus' presence is in inner healing where we lead a person to experience Him in past memories (see below). He has promised to never leave us or forsake us (see Heb. 13:5) and to be with us always (Matt. 28:20). So we ask the Holy Spirit to enable people through mental picturing to see and experience the truth that Jesus was with them even in difficult or abusive situations. I have seen hundreds of people brought to freedom from emotional and spiritual problems through experiencing truth in this way.

A major form of experiencing the truth lies in experiencing Jesus' nearness, whether in prayer, in difficult memories, in healing or deliverance, or in devotional or worship times. Many people are able to picture or feel Jesus ministering to them in their quiet times. He is there whether or not we can feel His presence. But feeling or picturing His nearness is a growth-producing way to experience the truth of His presence.

Experiencing true love whether from God or from humans would be another way of experiencing truth. We are told in Scripture that God is love (see 1 John 4:9) and whoever loves is from God (see 1 John 4:7). We are also told that our love is to be expressed in actions and in truth (see 1 John 3:18). It is primarily in actions that we experience the truth.

One important way to experience the truth of Jesus' presence is in worship. Churches that have given themselves to contemporary worship music have provided their congregations with a golden opportunity to get beyond the intellectual into the relational dimension of Christianity. Many actually experience Jesus as they worship. I believe contemporary worship is the most significant thing that has appeared in Christianity in the last couple of generations. Jesus told the Samaritan woman that there would come a time when people would worship "in spirit and in truth" (John 4:23). True worship is experiencing the truth of the presence of Jesus.

TRUE WORSHIP REQUIRES SPIRITUAL FREEDOM

But experiencing this kind of closeness to Jesus is one thing to those who live in emotional and spiritual freedom and quite another to those who are not free. Many Christians are not free to experience this kind of truth. They have accepted Christ into their lives and thus gained freedom from the penalty of sin, but they live in bondage to emotional and spiritual problems not automatically cleared up by their new relationship with Him.

This is where the lack of practicing spiritual power in our churches plays a role. Many (perhaps most) people don't get free from their bondages simply by coming to Christ. Over the years I have had a large number of dedicated Christians coming to my counseling office who stated that a major concern was that they could not feel close to Jesus. They knew they should be close to Him but didn't know how to get there. What we found in every case was that there were things in their life, usually in their childhood, that needed to be healed before they could be free to relate as they knew they should. These things may be spiritual, inherited from their ancestors, or emotional, the result of their reactions to mistreatment or misanalysis of childhood experiences.

This is where the missing dimension comes in. The lack of healing practice and power in our churches leaves people bound spiritually and emotionally. They may be gloriously saved but are not free. Freedom for most Christians is a step beyond salvation. It requires not just the presence of the Holy Spirit within but His freeing power to deal with the blockages. And it often requires the help of someone to guide the process we call "inner healing." But Jesus is always right there to enable the person to experience His healing power in dealing with emotional and spiritual issues that have been keeping the person from closeness to Jesus.

In inner healing our focus is on a person experiencing the presence of Jesus in past memories. For it is in the memories, usually held unconsciously, that the major blockages usually lie. Memories are like capsules holding within them the facts plus the feelings and reactions to past hurts of one kind or another. The facts cannot be changed, but the feelings can by responding to Jesus as He invites us to come to Him with our heavy burdens (see Matt. 11:28) and promises rest and peace when we give the burdens to Him.

Memory specialists tell us that we hold life experiences in memory pictures. This type of long-term memory is called *episodic memory*[2]. This being true, we find that gaining healing in these memory pictures works best when we can go back to the mental pictures and help the person to experience Jesus in the memories. The Holy Spirit empowers us to find the memories, usually through picturing, and then to give to Jesus the hurts held in those memory capsules. As we have led people to do this, we have seen hundreds gain emotional and spiritual freedom through experiencing Jesus in this way—freedom to live the life Jesus promised and freedom to relate to Jesus as He promised we could (see John 15:4-8).

Since Jesus is omnipresent, we lead people to experience His presence in their memories and to receive His healing as they give Him their damaged feelings and forgive those who have hurt them. Then in a new relationship with Him, they are in a position to enjoy our Savior who has promised to never leave us or forsake us and to be with us always to the end of time.

THE MISSING DIMENSION

Knowledge-oriented Christianity is anemic and powerless. I practiced that kind of Christianity for the first 38 years of my Christian experience—and it felt good. I've enjoyed my life as a Christian both before and after I became a "professional" Christian. But a whole new experience was mine when I moved into the area of spiritual power. When I began to see healing and deliverance happen to and then through me, I began to understand that something had been missing in my Christian experience.

I had been practicing an unbalanced Christianity, overemphasizing the cognitive truth part, stating but not focusing enough on the relational part, and virtually ignoring the spiritual part that was so important in Jesus' ministry.

This is the kind of Christianity I took to Nigeria. I was culturally sensitive, and there was a variety of other factors that combined to make my church planting efforts numerically successful. But since I knew nothing of the spiritual power part of the gospel, the Christians continued to go to their shamans for power even as they sincerely embraced the new faith. Theirs was what I have labeled a "dual allegiance" Christianity, where they went to church on Sunday but to shamans when they needed help because the wonderful miracle worker they heard about on Sundays didn't exist for them. Like most of us American Evangelicals, theirs was and is a two-dimensional Christianity with the third dimension missing.

TOWARD A THREE-DIMENSIONAL CHRISTIANITY

Discovering and experiencing this dimension in my own life, however, posed another problem for me. It was that I might overemphasize the exciting power dimension as I once had overemphasized the knowledge dimension. It is easy to go to either extreme if one is not careful to seek balance.

As I pondered this danger, then, I began to give attention to the need to retain the emphasis on truth that I had learned from my Evangelical teachers even as I learned more and more cognitively and experientially about spiritual power. But in this quest it became clear that the relational component was of even greater importance than the two emphases I was trying to balance. For we are not saved by either truth or power, only through a relationship with Jesus Christ. And we are expected to grow in that relationship to become more and more like Jesus. This is the aim of Christian experience.

As I have pointed out previously, the importance of relationship was known and preached. However, it has seldom received the emphasis it deserves, given its importance. We are taught about relating to Jesus but pretty much left to work out that relationship on our own. Why?

Here's where the need for spiritual power to produce freedom comes in. The ability to experience the intimacy with Jesus that we seek is dependent on living in freedom from spiritual and emotional hindrances. Jesus says He came to set captives free and to rescue His people from the enemy (see Luke 4:18-19). The enemy works on and within us to hinder that freedom, largely through attaching himself to emotional and spiritual problems. Only through working in Jesus' power, then, can the large numbers of Jesus' people who are in captivity be set free and thus enabled to relate intimately with Jesus.

Understanding and practicing a three-dimensional Christianity makes it possible for people to gain freedom from the hindrances to relationship that keep them in bondage. Freedom enables all to relate intimately with the true God and Savior, worshiping Him in spirit and in truth (see John 4:23). Let's make sure the "missing dimension" is a part of our powerful Christian experience.

ENDNOTES

1. C.H. Kraft, *Confronting Powerless Christianity* (Grand Rapids, MI: Chosen/Baker, 2002).

2. Daniel Schacter, *Searching for Memory* (New York: Basic Books, 1996).

Chapter 9

REALLY ... WHAT WOULD JESUS DO?

❧

MARCUS LAWSON

M arcus Lawson is the founder of North Gate Church and Mighty Warrior Ministries. He and his wife, Linda, have spent 28 years in full-time ministry. Their passion is to do "church as unusual," exposing people to God's presence and power in a form that is culturally relevant but untraditional and without compromise. They desire to see the Body "do the works of ministry" Jesus spoke of in John 14:12 including miracles, signs, wonders, and healing as part of a Kingdom lifestyle. Marc's passion is to see a revolution come to the American church culture as believers realize that God is not restricted to moving only in church services but that saints can live this supernatural lifestyle wherever they are—home, work, school, and in the marketplace!

Marc is the author of, *It's the End of the Church As We Know It—The 166 Factor*, which describes and encourages this change in church culture.

Marc and Linda have a vision to see Atlanta, Georgia, be one of the first major metro regions in America transformed by the presence of the Lord. In addition they have a burden for the family and the power of trans-generational revival.

Marc's intriguing discussion about what Jesus would *really* do follows:

POPULAR...BUT WRONG!

There is a popular trend that has so permeated the American church culture that it must be confronted straight on if we are to see an authentic move of God's power in our land. The reason I say this is because we must be clear on what "the real" is so as to experience it. This popular theology also must be held up to the light of the Scripture and examined with the primary means Jesus told us to use to determine whether something is of God and the Spirit or not. The question: "Does it bear fruit and is it good fruit?" In Matthew 7:17-20 Jesus speaks of this method of inspection:

> *Even so, every good tree bears good fruit, but a bad tree bears bad fruit. A good tree cannot bear bad fruit, nor can a bad tree bear good fruit. Every tree that does not bear good fruit is cut down and thrown into the fire. Therefore by their fruits you will know them.*

Unfortunately, this objective, unbiased, and even scientific criteria for determining whether God is truly "in" or "behind" things is rarely used by church leaders. Typically most leaders and believers weigh things by the American business definition of success: high and increasing numbers of people, greater income, and good press coverage. While these indicators may be a result of good fruit, they are not necessarily the fruit itself.

All things that grow quickly or become large and popular may not even be a success in God's view. One only need take a look at the American housing and financial markets recently and we see this truth, that simply because something becomes huge and pervasive doesn't mean it is built on a stable foundation. The prevailing line of thinking isn't always the correct one. And just because something has name recognition doesn't necessarily mean it is a sign of God's approval or His strategy. Crowds or a lack of them are not indicators that "God is with us." Jesus' biggest crowds left as quickly as they came. Sometimes the Lord blesses things He won't even inhabit.

ANOTHER GOSPEL

I marvel that you are turning away so soon from Him who called you in the grace of Christ, to a different gospel, which is not another; but there are some who trouble you and want to pervert the gospel of Christ (Galatians 1:6-7).

Most of us know of the phenomenal popularity of the *What Would Jesus Do* concept, based on the book by Charles Sheldon, *In His Steps*, written at the end of the 19th century. It advocates what I will call the "social gospel," for lack of a better term. By *social gospel* I mean feeding the poor, giving blankets to those needing warmth, finding shelter for those in need, and the like. Mr. Sheldon suggests (with great receptivity) that if He was physically among us today,

Jesus would pass out canned food, bring blankets to the homeless, and help the poor with natural things *rather than* spiritual things. The author presents the view that doing these kinds of " good works" was what Jesus meant when He said that His followers would do "greater works" (see John 14:12). Ultimately it was this book's philosophy that caused the popularity of the WWJD wristbands, bibles, and other items.

While believers extending kindness to the "least of these" is biblically right, proper, and our heart's inclination, we must do these acts in a context where the gospel is proclaimed, the sick healed, and the lame made to walk! When we don't, we foster a culture where there is the "social" without the "gospel." I am concerned this is where this line of thinking has led and is now accepted as "truth."

Charles Sheldon left this "social gospel" legacy that people should do works of kindness and niceness *rather than preach*. He can be credited with creating an alternative for Christians to avoid preaching or confronting the lost with the gospel. This unbalanced emphasis of equating social service with gospel preaching has *to this day* allowed many believers a "way out" of their biblical responsibility to preach to every creature. Based on a few obscure Gospel passages pulled out of context, this way of thinking has become popular among most Christians. While his motives were charitable, his conclusions could not be farther from the truth.

Of course, I am not saying that we should ignore the poor. On the contrary, it is good, right, and kind to remember the poor, to feed and help them. The apostle Paul reminds us to remember them in Galatians 2:10, and we should not neglect or forget them. But isn't this kind of mercy outreach obvious and an example of brotherly kindness? Isn't that what the parable of the Good Samaritan was all about—don't ignore the less fortunate or cast a blind eye to the needy? While many will be incensed and offended at the thought, Jesus didn't single out the poor as His favorite and only people group to shelter, clothe, and feed. He didn't command us to *feed* the poor,

He commanded us to *preach* to them. He also pointed out that the poor will be particularly receptive to the gospel message. Jesus cast out demons from and healed and preached to many poor people.

Much of the Church has subtly allowed this shift of thinking to happen; that this "social gospel is really preaching to the poor" especially among those churches that don't believe the gifts of the Spirit are necessary today. This "doing good deeds" without a Kingdom purpose or expectation of seeing God's power leaves the church in danger of becoming a community organization without a message that changes.

One clearly recognizable Christian movement we all greatly admire illustrates this point.

The Salvation Army was birthed by the powerful desire of William Booth to get out of the pew and into the streets to "preach the gospel to the poor." Booth was considered a heretic by many just because he wanted to preach and declare the gospel message and take the Scriptures *outside the church building*. Consider one of his quotes:

> While women weep, as they do now, I'll Fight; while little children go hungry, as they do now, I'll Fight; while men go to prison, in and out, in and out, as they do now, I'll Fight; while there is a poor lost girl upon the streets, while there remains one dark soul without the light of God, I'll Fight, I'll fight to the very end![2]
> —WILLIAM BOOTH

His gospel ministry began with fiery street preaching to the most downtrodden people; and consequently, aid to the poor *was a by-product*. William Booth's goal was to preach to the poor and give aid while directing them to churches. There was no way they could preach to the poor without wanting to assist them with their daily struggles regarding hunger, shelter, and clothing. In time it became apparent that the "street people" they won to Christ did not feel comfortable attending the existing churches. So they opened churches and even homes to take care of the homeless and hungry.

As time passed they set up centers in every city where they were preaching. Street-preaching workers reaching the lost were, in time, replaced by bell-ringing workers eager to receive offerings. Eventually this historic and revolutionary evangelistic ministry became more of a social service center for the poor where food and clothes were given away and the gospel proclaimed only in the churches they established.

The Salvation Army morphed into an exceptional social service agency, one of the largest on earth. While its kindness is legendary and its history honorable, the spiritual fruit in their outreaches is now a by-product instead of the goal. This is not an indictment, but an example *that the pure and simple effectiveness of preaching the gospel in power can be cast aside by its sheer success and the fruit it produces.* In my opinion, this organization today bears little resemblance to what is was when it was started. To quote an old friend of mine, Larry Tomczak, "Our history does not guarantee our destiny."

BE NICE OR TELL THE TRUTH?

At a conference in Atlanta a few years ago, I heard the incredible testimony of a Bulgarian apostle who had been beaten, arrested, and deported for preaching in his homeland before communism fell. He told amazing stories of miraculous protection from the horrific persecution he and the Bulgarian church experienced under communism. As he was preaching, he interjected this question, "What is it with you Americans about being nice? *Nice* is not a fruit of the Spirit, and Jesus never said, 'Go and be nice.'" This really got me thinking!

We in America have an affinity to want to come across as being "nice." Yet there is not one example in Scripture where Jesus taught about being nice or even acting nice. Jesus never said in the Sermon on the Mount, "Blessed are the nice. . . ." Being nice is not the same as preaching the gospel and could be one of the reasons we don't. We tend to think that God views things as we do, that love is somehow expressed in just being nice.

And we are so concerned that we might "turn someone off" when we share the gospel that we forget the power the authentic gospel has to set people free and set them on fire for God! Dumbing down our message to make it palatable is cowardly, compromising, ineffective, and produces bad results (fruit). The lesson should be obvious: God's ways really aren't our ways.

> *"For My thoughts are not your thoughts, nor are your ways My ways," says the Lord. "For as the heavens are higher than the earth, so are My ways higher than your ways, and My thoughts than your thoughts"* (Isaiah 55:8-9).

GOOD MOTIVES

We have been erroneously taught that if we do good things and our motives are good and right, God will bless it and us. Unfortunately that is just simply not true. The truth is Jesus only did that which the Father told Him to do. What outwardly may appear to look effective, kind, and good may not be fruitful or even that helpful! Jesus said things like, "preach the gospel to the poor." He also said, "Blessed are the poor in spirit, for theirs is the kingdom of heaven." There is a clear pattern Jesus followed as revealed to Him by His Father and it worked. We need to see that the method He used and the way He preached was always superior in its effects and bore much more fruit than any other way to present the gospel that we might dream up. Simply having good motives and a charitable heart doesn't guarantee the fruit we bear will be good or lasting nor does it equate to effective ministry based on Jesus' model.

SO WHAT *WOULD* JESUS DO?

If Jesus was on the streets right now in 21st-century suburban or urban America, would He hand out wristbands, give away sandwiches, and pass out cold water on street corners? Or would He bind up broken hearts, preach, cast out demons, and heal the sick? Would He go on television and plead for folks to send in money saying, "We'll go off the air if you don't give a pledge"... or would He multiply loaves and fish? Would He pass out tracts or would He bring life and freedom through His living Word? I think in our hearts we know the answers! Jesus *would* do and *did* do what He saw His Father doing and what we read about all through the New Testament.

Many of our attempts at ministry are in many ways missing the point of the example of Jesus' lifestyle. None of these "social gospel" activities are in themselves necessarily wrong, yet when they become a substitute for our primary mandate on the earth, they are out of order. Our lack of love or our cowardice to confront cannot allow us to whittle down our message to where we eventually don't even have one!

> Then Jesus answered and said to them, "Most assuredly, I say to you, the Son can do nothing of Himself, but what He sees the Father do; for whatever He does, the Son also does in like manner. For the Father loves the Son, and shows Him all things that He Himself does; and He will show Him greater works than these, that you may marvel. For as the Father raises the dead and gives life to them, even so the Son gives life to whom He will" (John 5:19-21).

Jesus' Priorities

If you are still unclear, look at the priorities of Jesus, or how He spent His time in ministry. Was His ministry primarily one of "feeding the poor" or "preaching to the poor"? They are *not* the same. Did He pass out meals and water? Jesus did feed the 5,000, but only after they stayed around for three days listening to Him teach and preach about the Kingdom! I think He felt it was the least He could do after they showed Him such commitment. Was He more concerned with giving them fish? Or teaching them how to be "fishers of men"?

And what about the time when Jesus said to Peter three times, "Feed My sheep"? Did He mean for Peter to literally give His followers food, or was He referring to the real food He had already referred to in the Gospel—to do His Father's will?

> But He said to them, "I have food to eat that you do not know about." So the disciples were saying to one another, "No one brought Him anything to eat, did he?" Jesus said to them, "My food is to do the will of Him who sent Me, and to accomplish His work (John 4:32-34 NASB).

If you ever think, *I wonder what Jesus really would do?*, then look in the Scripture at how He spent His time and at His priorities. A simple analysis of the Gospels shows He spent approximately one-third of His ministry time preaching and teaching the gospel of the Kingdom, mainly to His disciples; another third He spent casting out demons and doing miracles; and a third, He spent healing the sick.

Instead of adopting the latest politically correct Christian fad we find on the shelf of the local Christian bookstore, perhaps we should let the Word of God define our priority for us. Even if *everyone* is reading it or doing it, that doesn't make something true. There is so much information coming at Christians today that it would benefit most of us to go back and *read the Bible.* Many of us have become so spiritually lazy that we have become dependent on others to tell us what God is saying and what He means.

Jesus said that the things of the Kingdom would be so simple that a child could understand them! Romans 3:4 says, "Indeed, let God be true but every man a liar."

WHAT JESUS REALLY DID

Here are some Scriptures that teach what Jesus really did, not what Jesus *might* have done. These Scriptures are exceedingly clear—they say what they mean and mean what they say describing Jesus' activities as He preached the gospel of the Kingdom and performed miracles. This was Jesus' lifestyle in His day-to-day life. They include, but weren't centered on, a synagogue meeting or services. In fact, many of His most significant miracles and healings happened as He was "on the way" to somewhere else.

> *You know of Jesus of Nazareth, how God anointed Him with the Holy Spirit and with power, and how* **He went about doing good, and healing all who were oppressed by the devil;** *for God was with Him* (Acts 10:38 NASB).

> *When Jesus departed from there, two blind men followed Him, crying out and saying, "Son of David, have mercy on us!" And when He had come into the house, the blind men came to Him. And Jesus said to them, "Do you believe that I am able to do this?" They said to Him, "Yes, Lord." Then He touched their eyes, saying, "According to your faith let it be to you." And their eyes were opened. And Jesus sternly warned them, saying, "See that no one knows it."*

But when they had departed, they spread the news about Him in all that country. As they went out, behold, they brought to Him a man, mute and demon-possessed. And when the demon was cast out, the mute spoke. And the multitudes marveled, saying, "It was never seen like this in Israel!" (Matthew 9:27-33)

Now when He was in Jerusalem at the Passover, during the feast, many believed in His name when they saw the signs which He did (John 2:23).

Now a certain man was there who had an infirmity thirty-eight years. When Jesus saw him lying there, and knew that he already had been in that condition a long time, He said to him, "Do you want to be made well?" The sick man answered Him, "Sir, I have no man to put me into the pool when the water is stirred up; but while I am coming, another steps down before me."

Jesus said to him, "Rise, take up your bed and walk." And immediately the man was made well, took up his bed, and walked. And that day was the Sabbath (John 5:5-9).

And for this reason the Jews persecuted Jesus, and sought to kill Him because He had done these things on the Sabbath. But Jesus answered them, "My Father has been working until now, and I have been working" (John 5:16-17).

It certainly appears by these passages that Jesus performed a great number of signs, wonders, and miracles that He refers to as His "good works." So how then can we substitute this popular "social gospel" for Jesus' definition of good works that we are commanded to do?

> *But realize this, that in the last days difficult times will come. For men will be lovers of self, lovers of money, boastful, arrogant, revilers, disobedient to parents, ungrateful, unholy, unloving, irreconcilable, malicious gossips, without self-control, brutal, haters of good, treacherous, reckless, conceited, lovers of pleasure rather than lovers of God; holding to a form of godliness, although they have denied its power; avoid such men as these* (2 Timothy 3:1-5 NASB).

Isn't this exactly how the enemy operates? Doesn't he try to water down the truth about these good works of power, healing, and deliverance?

Healing cancer patients and seeing drug addicts delivered—isn't that "preaching the good news"? And binding up the broken-hearted—isn't that doing "good works"?

Why *wouldn't* the enemy's number-one strategy be to get Christians debating over whether or not to preach the gospel and even arguing over "how it is done"? The enemy of our soul has taken entire denominations and movements captive with this delusion, some even labeling anyone truly "doing what Jesus would do" deceived or into the occult. The enemy has sent the church on many bunny trails. There are many ministries pursuing anything and everything, *except* preaching the good news of the Kingdom. There are so many diversions, detours, and excuses for not preaching that it's obvious that the enemy is propelling all this fruitless activity forward. *The enemy wants the church caught up in obsessive activity that leads to nowhere and accomplishes nothing.* He is more than happy to encourage us in those directions.

WHAT *WOULDN'T* JESUS DO?

If we look in the New Testament and simply study Jesus' lifestyle for our model of ministry, we will also see what Jesus probably *wouldn't* do. The Gospel narratives of Christ's life give us a clear picture. Instead of buying into what is served up in Christian pop culture, we should learn from the chronicle of Jesus' life in the Gospels.

If He was here now, He probably *wouldn't* express His love for humanity by *only* doing these following things, as kind and as helpful as they may appear to us:

- Bring a team of His carpenter friends to your house for an Extreme Home Makeover.
- Hand out glasses of cold water at Interstate exit ramps.
- Wash your car.
- Mow your grass.
- Hand out turkeys on Thanksgiving and Christmas.
- Give you a bag of old clothes.
- Give you His old furniture or old shoes.
- Sell you donuts.
- Sell you cookies.
- Pat you on the back.
- Hand you a gospel tract.
- Sew doilies and mail them to prisoners.
- Give you a car.
- Wash your hair and do your nails.
- Teach English classes.

While all of these are generous, kind gestures and can be done to others in a right spirit, I humorously and facetiously mention them only to illustrate the point of how far our present Christianity has strayed from our prime mandate! I mean, did Jesus really die on the cross so we could do this kind of stuff? Is this the best He has for us?

The church now has 1,001 diversions that take us away from the prime mission of the church: to preach the gospel and make disciples (see Matt. 28:19). Jesus makes it clear that showing mercy and "doing to the least of these" should be part of every believer's lifestyle (see Matt. 25:35-40; 1 Cor. 13:2). However, to equate a "silent" mercy ministry with preaching, or to equate extending kindness in a Gospel vacuum with making disciples—THAT is unbalanced and the point of this article.

We have recently been spending time with several of the leaders of the Iris Ministries team led by Rolland and Heidi Baker and have been able to see this balance between bringing the gospel message with power and also the necessity to help converts with daily needs. It appears that when other believers see the immense success of their ministry and hear stories of how they lavishly show love to the children in their schools, people leave their meetings thinking that all they need do is hug somebody and then they will have conquered a nation! Of course it is more involved than that.

Many times we Americans only want the newest formula that takes the least amount of effort. Most of these works of kindness from this "social gospel" don't require any long-term involvement of relationship. In my church's weekly outreaches, many of the people we preach to or who get healed or delivered need a sustained discipleship relationship. "Drive-by" good deeds won't cut it if we want long-term results.

The people of Iris Ministries, for example, have devoted their lives to ministering to entire people groups, and without power they couldn't succeed. Of course they do attend to individual human needs as well.

So how can each of us make this our lifestyle? Jesus preached with demonstrations of power present each time, to illustrate and reveal the love of the Father to a lost and dying world! While "random acts of kindness" bless people and are encouraging, there can be *no substitute* for the power of the message of the Kingdom to deliver people! As a man named Peter Lord often said, "Keep the main thing the main thing."

Jesus healed the sick, cast out demons, and preached the message of the Kingdom. His message was crystal clear, His mission was without ambiguity, and His focus was laser accurate. He was and IS love in skin! He was born into our world as the firstborn of a new race who would walk as sons and daughters of God. He had power and authority over His circumstances and took dominion over everything He encountered. Unless the Father sent it, Jesus didn't receive it and wasn't distracted by it.

> *For those whom He foreknew, He also predestined to become conformed to the image of His Son, so that He would be the firstborn among many brethren* (Romans 8:29 NASB).

The way we change is clear in these and other passages of Scripture. The first way is to *repent*—to "change our mind." Jesus says in Matthew 4:17, *"Repent, for the kingdom of heaven is at hand."* Change comes when we repent or change our mind. *Repentance* in the Greek root means to "think differently." Changing the way you think will change the way you live. "For as he thinks in his heart, so is he" (Prov. 23:7). Many Christians know the truth only in their minds, not hearts. They are agnostic in their hearts.

The second way we change is through beholding and being transformed into *His* image, not by attempting to fix ourselves! Second Corinthians 3:17-18 says, *"Now the Lord is the Spirit; and where the Spirit of the Lord is, there is liberty. But we all, with unveiled face beholding as in a mirror the glory of the Lord, are being transformed into the same image from glory to glory, just as by the Spirit of the Lord."*

While some theologians hold to a view that due to man's deep depravity we can scarcely (or not at all) share His divine character, the Bible is quite clear that God's prescription for our deliverance involves doing the works He did as well as walking as He did. First John 2:6 says, *"The one who says he abides in Him ought himself to walk in the same manner as He walked"* (NLT). To be a new creature in Christ requires us to believe and act as though that "old man" is dead. He wouldn't command us to do something that we were too bad to do!

If looking to Jesus and getting our eyes off ourselves is the key to our transformation, then obsessing over our faults and failings is a dead-end street. The obsession over self-improvement is a road to nowhere. Transformation occurs through beholding Him, not our flesh! The Spirit changes us, not self-improvement techniques or discipline. Jesus never required the apostles to do anything but to follow Him and *imitate* Him. He was mentoring them as they beheld what He was and what He did. He modeled a new way of living and He told them (and us) "greater things than this, you can do!" It is possible for all of us to do these things if we keep our eyes on our primary purpose—to bring Jesus' Kingdom to the lost, the lame, the deaf, the blind through a demonstration of His power and love! Surely we are to also extend kindness with daily needs and that will be obvious to us as we go along.

Do you believe what He said and do you want to do the same? You can! And if you will only believe, you will!

ENDNOTES

1. K. Connie Kang, "Pentecostalism Enthusiasm is Spreading," http://articles.latimes.com/2006/apr/28/local/me-spirit28; accessed 9/26/08.

2. http://thinkexist.com/quotation/while_women_weep-as_they_do_now-i-ll_fight-while/333335.html; accessed 9/26/08.

Chapter 10

STILL ASTONISHED BY JESUS

⟨୨୨ᕕ℃ℓ⟩

DENNY CLINE

Denny and his wife, Ann, have pastored in Oregon for 20 years. With a team of 27 adults, they planted the Albany Vineyard in 1994, where Denny continues to serve as senior pastor. They have been privileged to experience several awesome visitations of the Holy Spirit, impacting youth and adults alike with healing, salvation, and deliverance.

Denny is known and loved for his simple, compassionate, and yet extravagant approach to Kingdom life. A notorious "God-chaser," he has also led the Albany Vineyard in a bold direction that has birthed many developing ministries and produced a rich harvest of fathers, mothers, and children filled with the zeal of the Lord.

The Vineyard is an expanding resource church that emphasizes love, worship, the presence of God, and the importance of all the saints participating in ministry. It is Denny and Ann's dream to see thousands of people become carriers of God's glory to their neighbors, work places, and the nations.

ASTONISHED BY JESUS

When was the last time you were astonished? In our modern, Western culture, things change so fast even the meaning of the word *astonished* is lost on the newest, the latest, the most popular. By astonished, I mean, being moved to the core of our beings, in a way that challenges our paradigm for living. Even the church in the Western world has often settled for what is *culturally current* as a way of trying to draw people to Jesus. Yet Jesus moved people with His presence, as Emmanuel—God with us.

Things have changed in our society. We are called a "post modern" culture that has doubts about absolute truth, morality, and a certain future. The Bible is not readily accepted as *God's Word* by many in today's Western world, as it was in times past. Consequently, the meaning of spirituality, church, God, and Christ are not as easily communicated through rational argument or persuasion. Therefore, what the apostle Paul said shouldn't surprise us, *"...my speech and my preaching were not with persuasive words of human wisdom, but in demonstration of the Spirit and of power, that your faith should not be in the wisdom of men but in the power of God* (1 Cor. 2:4-5).

The gospel has always been a gospel of *power* and *demonstration.* Jesus as the pioneer of our salvation modeled how to communicate the gospel in word and deed. His teachings were powerful and often backed up by a demonstration in healing, signs and wonders, and miracles. The same signs that followed Jesus were meant to follow His disciples.

It takes faith to believe in what is *humanly impossible*. But that's the point, really. Salvation is humanly impossible; that is, the restoration of sinful man to a Holy God. Miracles and salvation take faith in the power of an eternal God.

Living lives of faith—desiring the unseen realm to burst into the natural world—takes a pioneering heart; sometimes leading us on a strange journey. From the very moment I was baptized in the Holy Spirit, I was faced with choices to either live in the supernatural by faith, or ignore the new reality of the presence of God in my life. Surely it must be so for everyone who encounters the Holy Spirit in such a life-transforming way.

From my initial encounter with the Holy Spirit I began to experience dreams, visions, and a desire to see the Kingdom manifest on earth as it must surely be in Heaven. The power of the gospel became a new reality and ever-present desire in my heart. From that time my desire has been to see people healed, delivered, saved, and transformed by the same Spirit that raised Christ from the dead. Only more recently, in this decade, has the idea of the dead being raised in the Western world been a desire of mine as well. Why? Because it is in the list of those works that Jesus commanded His disciples to do.

These are the very works that not only still astonish, but also wake up a rational Western world to the reality of God's presence on earth—the King and His Kingdom. So let me share a few parts of my journey as an everyday pastor, serving the Body of Christ, and most importantly, Jesus, as one of His followers.

THE POWER OF GOD

I will never forget a weekend a few years ago after a wonderful time with youth from all over our region. Two young men who had given their lives to Christ only months earlier went late at night to a pool hall to get something to eat. It was the only place open that had food at midnight in our city. As they ordered their food at the bar, two other young men began taunting them from across the room, yelling expletives that are common in pro-wrestling matches. Our two young men yelled back to them, "Give us a God yeah!"

The drunk and boisterous guys came over to them with not-so-good intentions, wanting to know what they were saying. "We said, 'Give us a God yeah!'" When they heard them say it this time, it was as if the words fell like a hammer on their hearts; they went down to their knees weeping. By this time, the owner and tender of the bar was quite concerned that he had a situation on his hands.

The server had a different take. She had watched one of our small groups meet in that same area, sharing the Word, and fellowshipping for a year. She recognized what was happening and said, "Leave them alone; it's God!" The next morning in our Sunday service, when an invitation was given to receive Christ, these two, now very sober young men, came forward, fell into my and my wife's arms, and with tears gave their lives to Christ.

It didn't stop there. The following Tuesday I went to a new place downtown to get a haircut from a young man my daughter recommended. I honestly had no intention of talking to him about anything, let alone God. I know that's not a good attitude for a pastor, but I simply thought I was getting a haircut from someone who would cut my hair, not chew on my ear for a change. Wrong again. The young man asked me my vocation. I felt embarrassed that I was only selfishly there to get my haircut and not really interested in him.

After telling him I was a pastor, I thought, *I should invite him to our weekly meeting at the pool hall*. When I invited him and named the pool hall, to my astonishment, I looked in the mirror as the young man began to stagger and tears filled his eyes. "What's wrong?" I asked, "Are you OK?"

He responded, "No, I don't think so. When you said the name of the pool hall, something hot went all through my body. My brother said he had a similar experience Saturday night at the pool hall and wants to tell me about it tonight!"

Not only was this man astonished, but so was I. He had a three-day visitation from the Lord after that, and gave his life to Christ. Months later so did his once-atheist wife. They both began attending a Baptist church that believes in the power of the Holy Spirit a few hours away from us.

If we are ashamed of the message, perhaps in part it is because at times we don't see a demonstration of power to follow. The apostle Paul states in Romans 1:16 that he is not ashamed of the gospel, because it is the power of God unto salvation for everyone who believes. The gospel was designed to be preached and confirmed with signs and wonders following. Instead of asking why power is lacking or inconsistent, it seems easier to come up with a rationale suggesting it is not important in our modern world. If that was true, people would be much more interested in our message and less interested in seeking answers to life's questions from other sources of power: psychics, spiritualists, and New Age healers.

If the early church and even Jesus felt it was important to demonstrate the Kingdom, how much more important is it in today's world that is skeptical, prideful, and humanistic? The message of the gospel is the hope of the Kingdom of Heaven made manifest on the earth. In a time to come, there will be a new Heaven and new earth. This is because all the kingdoms of the world will yield to the Kingdom of our Lord and Christ. This new Kingdom is a heavenly Kingdom filled with heavenly blessings. How can the church persuade people in darkness who believe in the philosophies, religions, and practices of the world system without a demonstration of a Kingdom that has the power to transform lives?

Over the next couple of years, I became good friends with the young man I mentioned previously. He truly became a new creation in Christ. His encounter with Jesus changed him from inside out. It challenged him to look at every part of his life and begin a journey of transformation through the Word and the Spirit of God. As I watched him grow, I recalled childhood friends who, later on in life, came to Christ in similar ways. This led me to think about the stark contrast of the beginning of my own Christian journey.

BEGINNINGS

Out of God's sovereignty, I was pulled into Christianity during the Jesus Movement in a time of great questioning and upheaval, during the early 1970s. Like many of my friends, I was caught up in rebellion, strange philosophies, and the experimentation of our day. Because of the unrest and uncertainty of that time, I was searching for answers and truth. Like many of my generation, I read *Late Great Planet Earth* by Hal Lindsey. Whether one agrees or disagrees with the eschatology, God used that book to grab my attention and many of my peers.

Consequently, I asked Christ to forgive my sins and reserve my place in Heaven. Unfortunately, there was no power encounter, no exposure to the fullness of salvation, or introduction to the teaching of the gospel of the Kingdom of Heaven. Sadly, I had no exposure to the church either. What I did have were lots of friends in the same situation, and tapes from a dispensational teacher reinforcing our decision and our hope for a future in the afterlife. We had little to show us the way to a life-transforming relationship with the Holy Spirit, who has the power to set us apart and give us a supernatural life that includes healing for the soul and body.

I struggled to rid myself of bad habits, a selfish heart, and even became a victim of the earlier abuse of my body, with health issues usually reserved for more elderly folks. I had to know the God I asked to save me was real. I had to know if He really loved me and if He was bigger than the devils I had let into my life. I became so broken about this, in desperation I set aside nearly a year to seek His face to find out if He was who the Bible says He is.

It was toward the end of this season of being set apart to God, seeking to know Him as He really is, that I encountered the Holy Spirit. He is a person of power, who gives gifts and supernatural impartations to help live life as a follower of Jesus. However, I quickly realized it was not only for my own need, but also to help others and to reach those who don't know Christ.

Walking in the Spirit is the greatest adventure and most enjoyable way of life I can ever imagine. I can see why the early church, and those we read about throughout history, were willing to suffer, give up everything, and face anything to see that the gospel was spread far and wide. The present reality of the Kingdom of God in power is a very compelling force for those who experience it. The love of God is not just imagined, but shed abroad in our hearts by the Holy Spirit; this is the greatest motivator to live for over the course of a lifetime.

The God of all creation longs to continue to amaze us with kindness, love, and power encounters of all kinds. This is not only for our transformation, but to display His goodness to those who are trapped in darkness. I can't count the number of times Jesus has astonished me by healing people, meeting needs in miraculous ways, and speaking words that could only come from the God of Heaven.

I believe God wants to astonish us with His presence in personal encounters that come from the Holy Spirit and the realm of Heaven. But I also believe He wants to astonish entire cities and regions, even nations with what the Book of Acts calls, *unusual and extraordinary miracles* like those worked through the hands of Paul (see Acts 19:11).

I have witnessed many healings and miracles, except the raising of the dead. Jesus told His disciples in John 14:12 that those who believe in Him would do the works that He did and even greater works because of the outpouring of the Holy Spirit upon all humanity. The early church began to fulfill these words, yet many of these works are reserved for each succeeding generation to astonish and draw the multitudes to Christ.

Much of the church in today's Western world is focused on the social justice issues of the Kingdom message. That is an important aspect of communicating the love of God and revealing His nature and His Kingdom, but there are many Christian and non-Christian organizations that are focused only on social issues of the current culture and politics. Noble as that may seem, where is the power to transform life?

SUPERNATURAL WORKS

Jesus listed a number of supernatural works that He Himself performed and commanded His followers to do the same. Some of them are to heal the sick, cleanse the lepers, raise the dead, and cast out demons (see Matt. 10:8). And then there are those greater works that may be different, but from the same source of power, the Holy Spirit, that are for us. Paul laid his hands on handkerchiefs and sent them with people to place on their sick and bound friends—they were healed! (See Acts 19.) Astonishing. Peter's shadow passed over the sick and they were healed. (See Acts 5.)

If Jesus did such works, they were never recorded in the Gospels. Could He have done them? Of course. But we are called to *greater works*. The point is, Jesus Christ is the same yesterday, today, and forever; and there are many astonishing works to be worked through God's people to capture the attention of an unbelieving world with a demonstration of God's love and power.

I believe, and the Bible seems to agree with this notion, that the raising of the dead is one of the most compelling works of power that can not only astonish the unbelieving, but also affect entire cities and regions with the reality of a present Kingdom from Heaven. Paul is so adamant about this fact that he poses the question, "For if the dead do not rise, then Christ is not risen. And if Christ is not risen, your faith *is* futile; you are still in your sins" (see 1 Cor. 15:16-17)? Wow, what a stirring Scripture. The hope of every Christian rests upon the historical fact that Jesus Christ was raised from the dead by the power of the Holy Spirit. It is through the same Spirit dwelling in us that we have hope of eternal life.

I realize Paul was referring directly to the resurrection of Jesus in the passage to encourage the Corinthian church about those who had passed away. But think about what he is saying for our day. Are the dead raised? Does the God of yesterday still do miracles of astonishing power today? If not, our hope is solely in words and persuasive arguments, not power. We must simply believe a message passed down through centuries. Yes it's true that the message itself has power to change the lives of those who truly put their trust in the death and resurrection of Christ, having never seen Jesus or a resurrection. But what an astonishing reality and compelling argument for many who are skeptical when the dead are still raised! And the dead are still raised today. However, most reports of the dead being raised are from nations other than those of the Western world.

There may be many reasons for this, but it seems consistent with the Western mindset that unless it fits our rational and educational grid, as with other works of power, it is not to be expected. Even though the Pharisees believed in the resurrection to come; when Jesus raised Lazarus from the dead, it so challenged their thinking that they plotted how to put him to death. When Paul began to move in what the Bible calls extraordinary and unusual miracles, it included raising a young man from the dead. He then began to suffer great persecution in those regions. Why? The reality of the Kingdom in power ends all arguments, demanding a decision about Christ.

That's the kind of gospel I believe our Western world needs today. Our nation could be at a tipping point. We have been asking God to leave our nation in more and more ways over the last several decades. If we lose or deny the power of the Holy Spirit in the church as well, where will we be in the coming decades? Lord, rend the heavens and visit Your people with astonishing power in our day.

I close with these questions: How was the gospel preached or presented to you, and how did you receive it? Are you experiencing the life of a transforming gospel of power?

I'm not only referring to miracles, signs, and wonders, but power in every aspect of life: a new kind of living, the adventure of spiritual gifts, and the power to be a *living epistle* that draws others to a *living Christ*.

Chapter 11

POWER MINISTRY AND ENTRY INTO THE KINGDOM

PETER H. DAVIDS

P eter H. Davids was brought up Plymouth
Brethren in Syracuse, New York, and Lynch-
burg, Virginia. He graduated from Wheaton College
in 1968, Trinity Evangelical Divinity School in 1971,
and University of Manchester in 1974. He is ordained
in the Episcopal Church and has worked for seminaries of several denominations as well as served a
variety of churches.

Peter is presently Professor of Biblical Theology at
the trans-denominational St. Stephen's University in
New Brunswick, Canada, as well as a theological

advisor for the German-speaking Vineyard Movement, having previously served on its board. He is known for his part in the book *Hard Sayings of the Bible* (InterVarsity Press) as well as his commentaries on James, First and Second Peter, and Jude.

REPENT AND BELIEVE

Jesus started his ministry by announcing that God's kingdom (or, as a better translation more sensitive to contemporary culture has it, God's imperial rule) was present and that people were to "repent" and commit themselves to that message, that reality. "The time is fulfilled, and the kingdom of God has come near; repent, and believe in the good news" (Mark 1:15 NRSV).[1] The message was clear in the context of that culture: God was starting to directly express his rule over His creation; people were therefore to turn from their self-directedness and their loyalties to any other type of rule and submit to this imperial rule of God.

While we may think of "repent and believe" in a religious context and thus become introspective in terms of considering what sins we must repent from and what truths we must believe, N.T. Wright had shown that the Greek world pair underlying "repent" and "believe in" means to turn from one's past rebellion or loyalty and give one's loyalty another.[2] Thus people recognized that the good news was that God was starting to openly express His imperial rule and that they were being called to turn from past loyalties, personal or political, and give all their loyalty to this kingdom and submit to this rule. This message was underlined and authenticated by the exercise of divine power in healing people and driving out demons, i.e., in power ministry.

The big issue that was unclear at the beginning of the Gospel narrative was the relationship of Jesus to this rule of God. Was He a prophet announcing the event (which could include His giving signs that He was truly acting on God's behalf) or did He have a more significant role than this? That the latter was the case is hinted at in His call in Mark 1:17, "Follow Me," for He was calling people to follow Him personally and submit to His teaching rather than preparing them for some other leader or event as John the Baptist had (see Mark 1:7-8).

The debate about Jesus' role in this imperial rule would continue for some time; in Mark 8:28 we discover that popular opinion still identified Jesus with a prophetic figure (and He certainly was prophetic), but that His followers thought of Him as "the Messiah," God's anointed ruler through whom the rule of God would be expressed.[3] Thus power ministry was important in authenticating that Jesus had come from God, but in and of itself it was ambiguous.

This rule of God resulted in a new lifestyle. When one committed to Jesus as the one who expressed the rule of God, one submitted to His teaching. Otherwise the claim that He was the Messiah was so much hot air. If one was really committed to the belief that Jesus was God's spokesperson, then this implied submission to His teaching. This was even truer if He were not just a spokesperson for God but God's appointed ruler. Thus His followers both during His pre-crucifixion life and after His resurrection are called apprentices or trainees (traditionally translated "disciple").

The training included teaching about how one should live under the rule of God (e.g., the Sermon on the Mount), as one would expect if one were being naturalized into the life of a "foreign-to-you" nation, and the teaching itself was demonstrated by the Master, not as a "how I do this" instruction, but as a natural part of His lifestyle. If one were Jesus' follower or trainee, one lived like the Master lived (including traveling with Him)[4] and did what the Master did. His words were explanations of His behavior and His expectations of their behavior. That, of course, is just what one expected of a teacher or leader in those days. Those who were His trainees were those whom He considered part of His family. Mark 3:33-35 (NRSV) says: "And He replied, 'Who are My mother and My brothers?' And looking at those who sat around Him, He said, 'Here are My mother and My brothers! Whoever does the will of God is My brother and sister and mother.'"[5] It is clear that for Jesus His teaching was what expressed the will of God.

Thus a picture emerges. One listened to the words of Jesus and viewed His deeds, including those deeds that we consider deeds of power, and on this basis one decided that this Man was at least a prophet of God announcing a true message. Therefore one gave Jesus one's allegiance and started to change one's lifestyle to accord with His lifestyle (including His verbal teaching). That is how one came under the rule of God or became part of the Kingdom (to use the more metaphorical language). As one submitted to Him one might find him or herself caught up in participating in what Jesus was doing, whether that be getting folk into groups (see Mark 6:39) or handing out bread and fish that He has just broken (see Mark 6:41) or struggling in a boat when He comes striding by (see Mark 6:48).

Now it is true that He had His principle assistants that where generally in the center of anything that happened, yet surely the women who followed Him and others from the larger group were also involved in some of the events of His life. And while it is clear that the Twelve were singled out to be given power and sent out to reproduce Jesus' teaching and deeds (see Mark 6:6b-13), at least one Gospel indicates that other more ordinary trainees were also so commissioned (see Luke 10:1-12) and John's Gospel has Jesus predicting that this would be normal for His followers (see John 14:12-14). Thus we have the paradigmatic order: hear the good news, submit to the rule of God in Jesus, and take on the lifestyle of Jesus, including doing all the various types of works that He did.

We should notice, however, that the various parts of the

teaching of Jesus are not separable: when He told His followers to go out and proclaim the imperial rule of God, He not only promised them power, but he also instructed them to take risks: they go out as "lambs in the midst of wolves"; they are to be at material risk, since they take neither food nor money for the journey (see Luke 10:3); they are to accept the provision that comes to them and not seek to improve their social or material situation (see Luke 10:8); they will sometimes experience rejection (see Luke 10:10-11).[6] Jesus lived just such a risky, giving life; it fit with His demonstration of the power of God. His followers should also expect the lifestyle of risk and the experience of power to fit together.

DEATH IS NOT THE LAST WORD

It is clear that Jesus was executed by crucifixion by the Roman occupation forces on the basis of His having declared Himself to be God's ruler. The triumphal entry of Mark 11 had symbolism that was obvious enough to the natives of Palestine, but perhaps not to the Romans, and the question of the high priest that Jesus agreed to (see Mark 14:61) probably would not have been understood by the Romans,[7] but by the time Jesus is crucified, the Romans understand that this Man claimed to be the Jewish king (see Mark 15:2,9,12,18,26). Thus we come to the end of Mark 15 (and the parallel passages in the other Gospels), and God's designated ruler is dead.[8]

The Christian story, however, is that death is not the last word, but that God vindicated Jesus' claims by resurrecting Him. In fact, Paul claims, this is the heart of the Christian message without which the death of Jesus is meaningless (see 1 Cor. 15:14,17-18). It is not for no reason that the Apostles' Creed balances three lines about the death of Jesus with three lines about His resurrection, ascension, and session, for the first group without the second group would be meaningless. Now the question arises as to whether this death and resurrection changed anything about how one comes under the rule of God and what flows from this? Admittedly our materials are more difficult to deal with, for with the exception of Acts we are dealing with letters to groups of followers of Jesus. Because these people were already followers of Jesus they did not need the basic teaching that is found in the Gospels. The purpose of the letters is to solve this or that issue that arose later in this or that particular church in this or that cultural situation. However, we will see that the pattern of the Gospels is also found in those passages in the letters that refer to one's coming under the rule of God. We will look at several examples from different authors.

When it comes to how one comes under the rule of God, the key passage in Hebrews is 6:1-2: the "foundation" is described as: (1) *repentance*, (2) *commitment* (a better translation than "faith"), and then (3) *instruction* (probably followed by action on the basis of that instruction) on baptisms,[9] laying on of hands, resurrection of the dead, and eternal judgment. Resurrection (except that Jesus is already resurrected) and eternal judgment are clearly future, leaving baptism as a present possibility, so one has four parts to what we might call initiation into the community of the followers of Jesus. Interestingly enough the *result* of this initiation includes "sharing in the Holy Spirit" and "tasting...the power of the age to come." These are part of the package one receives when properly initiated, not optional add-ons. Thus the power of the Spirit should be viewed as a normal part of proper Christian initiation, at least according to Hebrews.

Turning to Acts, the basic passage is Acts 2:14-42.[10] This message first argues that "God has made Him both Lord and Messiah [i.e., ruler, king], this Jesus whom you crucified" and that the manifestation of the Holy Spirit is evidence of this fact. Those who are struck by this datum are called upon to turn from their old allegiances, submit to the Messiah Jesus in baptism, and then they too would receive the Holy Spirit. Afterward these people became trainees (thus their need for teaching by Jesus' delegates or by those passing on the teaching of Jesus' delegates) and thereby entered into the lifestyle (financial and practical sharing, celebration of the Lord's Supper as a meal, and prayers) of the community of Jesus' followers.

Here we have similar elements to those in Hebrews: a breaking with past allegiances and the lifestyles associated with them (repentance), a commitment to Jesus, an expression of this in baptism (in Hebrews, as noted in the note previous, there is a need for instruction to clarify the difference between that baptism in which one pledges oneself to Jesus and Jewish rites of purification or the baptism of John the Baptist or other Jewish groups), and the reception of the Holy Spirit, resulting in one's being part of the group that is submitted to Jesus and increasingly appropriates his lifestyle, including His power ministry (of which there are many examples in Acts).

PROCLAIMING THE GOOD NEWS

When it comes to his proclamation of the good news, Paul's key passage is Romans 10:9: "...if you confess with your lips that Jesus is Lord and believe in your heart that God raised Him from the dead, you will be saved."[11] While Paul only cites this basic proclamation incidentally as part of an argument that both Jews and Gentiles come under the rule of God in the same way ("the same Lord is Lord of all and is generous to all who call on Him"), it is a revealing statement. The basic confession that one makes in coming under the rule of God is "Jesus is Lord."

In a world in which the patriotic assertion was "Caesar is Lord" the meaning was clear. One had "repented" of other allegiances (whether to other divinities or to Caesar or to nationalisms) and had given one's allegiance to Jesus. This change of allegiance was not something done secretly or in one's heart, but one done before others "with your lips." Surely First Peter 3:21 is right to locate this

"pledge/appeal to God from a good conscience" (author's translation) as being part of baptism. Baptism is to life in Jesus as a
wedding is to life in marriage.[12] And it is clear that this is not a
pledge to follow the ideas of Jesus, but rather one to follow Jesus as
presently being Lord, for not only is a present tense verb probably
implied in Romans 10:9, but Paul also goes on to say that one must
be committed to the fact that God has raised Him from the dead.

Followers of Jesus are not following the ideals of a dead leader,
a set of teachings that He left behind (although of course they do
follow His teachings, for why should He repeat what He has already
taught). They are following a living ruler who "shall return to judge
the living and the dead" (as the Apostles' Creed puts it later). It is
also clear that Paul expects that experiences of the Holy Spirit will
be the result of such a commitment. Galatians 3:5 indicates that
miracles took place among the Galatian churches due to their
commitment to Jesus, and Galatians 5:22-25 indicates that the
same Spirit produces a new lifestyle. In fact, Paul says that those
who do not exhibit this lifestyle are not followers of Jesus at all, for
they are not led by the Spirit but by the unaided human nature (see
Gal. 5:19-21).

It is all of one piece: committing oneself to Jesus means coming
under His rule, which action implies that there is a new power in
one that produces a new lifestyle. The new lifestyle is not just an
ethical way of life, one modeled on how Jesus lived, but it is also a
way of acting in the world that includes manifesting the power of
God, whether that be through miracles or through other gifts of the
Spirit. One has been delivered (i.e., saved) from this age by coming
under the rule of God in Jesus (and remember that this was in
contrast to Caesar who was also called Savior in that he delivered the
empire from chaos, whether that be the chaos of bandits or the chaos
of foreign invasion, and brought them peace) and one lives as a
citizen of the coming age, manifesting the powers of the coming age
in all of how one lives.

Thus we have a paradigm like our previous paradigm. One listens to a message about Jesus (and sees a lifestyle in those proclaiming the message that is consistent with that message in every respect, including in the manifestation of the power of the coming age). On this basis one breaks his or her past allegiances and in their place commits to Jesus as Lord/ruler, expressing this commitment in baptism in which one takes a pledge of allegiance to Jesus. Because of this they receive God's Spirit that enables them to live the lifestyle of the Kingdom, including both what contemporary believers consider deeds of power and what they consider ethical living (but which is just as much deeds of power, for only the power of God can break the power of the human nature received at birth).

Therefore one adjusts all of their life to come into accord with the teaching of Jesus, for he or she is living in the expectation that Jesus will return to manifest His rule on earth and thus that they will face His judgment (and receive His commendation)[13] and they participate in His rule of this world.

A NEW RULER

The contemporary problem, however, is that this is not the understanding that people have when they "become a Christian" or "get saved." Usually they have no idea that Jesus is a ruler in contrast to whatever rule they have been living under, including the rule of the nation state in which they find themselves. They may be sorry for this or that deed, but rarely are they turning from their whole life-orientation to a totally new social and political orientation toward life. They may ask Jesus to do something about their guilt, their "sins," but only some are by that act committing themselves to live under His rule, to be directed by His teaching, in the expectation that in the end the whole of their life will be judged by that standard.

Baptism may be viewed as an optional (although important) "extra."[14] There may or may not be the expectation that on the basis of one's submission to Jesus as Lord one can expect God to empower one to live out his lifestyle. Often this is presented as something that is only inward ("You have the Spirit whether or not you experience anything") or a second (optional, although also important) stage, as is "discipleship" (that is sometimes thought of more as a commitment rather than an act of expressing the rule of God in this life). In other words, using the metaphor of "new birth" for this process either "gestation" has resulted in a "stillbirth" or the "birth process" has been faulty resulting in either a "new life" that is no life of the Kingdom at all, but a false promise, or a distorted life of the Kingdom that lacks the unified flow of kingdom rule in deeds of power of all types.[15]

Perhaps if we were again to capture the wholism of the good news as proclaimed in the New Testament and were to let that result in a Kingdom-oriented evangelistic process, the birthing of new members of the Kingdom would be so wholistic that power ministry and living like Jesus in other ways would again be a unity, one flowing out of the other into a risky lifestyle that sees "Satan fall from heaven like a flash of lightning" (Luke 10:18) and thinks it no great thing.

ENDNOTES

1. All other biblical texts cited in this chapter are from the New Revised Standard Version of the Bible unless noted otherwise.

2. N.T. Wright, *Jesus and the Victory of God* (Minneapolis: Fortress Press, 1996), 250-251. Wright argues this on the basis of Josephus' use of the pair in *Life* 110. This should not surprise us, for Rudolph Bultmann in his article on *pisteuô* in the Theological Dictionary of the New Testament, Vol. 6, pages 173-228, had already shown that words translated "believe" mean to "trust" or "commit to" when followed by the Greek dative or a word meaning "in."

3. I am purposely avoiding saying that there was a unitary concept of Messiah in the Judaisms of the first century. Some

Jewish groups did not expect any coming "Messiah" at all, while others only expected an anointed prophet, for they thought that God would intervene directly without mediation. Still others expected two anointed personages, one of Aaron and one of David, a priest and a king, often along with a prophet, so that all of the roles for which God had people anointed could be fulfilled. The Old Testament is far from clear on this subject and thus contemporary Judaisms were of multiple opinions. What is clear is that what Peter said on behalf of his colleagues is that they considered Jesus a royal anointed person, a ruler. We do not know all that they believed that Jesus should do as ruler nor do we know if Peter and his colleagues agreed on Jesus' job description or whether it was something that they debated around the campfire when Jesus was absent.

4. If we follow the Johannine chronology that has Jesus teaching for three years before His crucifixion, then it is likely that He did not travel in winter. Likewise, while some of His core followers did abandon their livelihoods and follow Him, others probably only did so for shorter periods of time. For instance, we know that some women followed Him around (see Luke 8:1-3), but for women who had small children this would have been impossible to do for any significant length of time, although they may well have been among the crowds that gathered when He came to town that followed Him outside of town (e.g., those who were present at the feeding of the 5,000).

5. This passage demonstrates Jesus preferring His "fictive family" (i.e., His non-blood family of followers) to His birth family, which is just what later followers of Jesus were expected to do: "leave father and mother and follow." It also tells us that neither His mother nor His siblings were His followers at this point in His ministry, although His mother for sure and possibly some if not all of His siblings were His followers by the time He was crucified. Paul informs us, for example, that Jesus appears to His brother

James right after His resurrection, which probably indicates that James was a follower before the crucifixion. Yet the prominence of Jesus' family after the resurrection was because they had become His followers *and* were His blood kin, not just because they were His blood kin.

6. Interestingly enough, the only one whom we know of who actually followed the instructions about what to do when one is rejected was Paul (see Acts 13:51), which indicates that Barnabas and he apparently felt that the instructions of Jesus were relevant to their post-resurrection ministry. If that is true, then we dare not restrict Jesus' teaching to His pre-crucifixion ministry, as comfortable and convenient as that might be for us.

7. Nor is it always understood by modern readers, who hear in "Son of the Blessed One" an ontological claim to be divine rather than a reference to Second Samuel 7 in which David's ruling son was promised adoption by God, as is seen in Psalm 2.

8. One has in Mark 15:39 the statement of the centurion, "Truly this man was God's Son!" Yet while it brackets the Gospel (see Mark 1:1) and is the confession of a Gentile, it is also a confession about a man who is now dead. It is said over Jesus' corpse. God's Son is dead.

9. The text has "baptisms" plural, most likely because one first had to be instructed on how baptism into Jesus differed from John's baptism (cf. Acts 19) and/or various Jewish ritual baths to remove impurity. Once one understood the difference, it would be natural to follow through with the baptism into Jesus.

10. The method of Acts is to explain something most fully the first time it appears and then only to explain what is new in subsequent occurrences. Thus the first proclamation of the good news is the fullest, while the other nine evangelistic sermons in Acts often abbreviate what is explained more fully in the earlier sermons and focus their attention on the new elements (e.g., Acts 17 focuses on the need in a pagan context to argue that there is only one God,

creator of Heaven and earth, before declaring Jesus to be His designated world ruler).

11. This argument is dependent upon N.T. Wright, *Paul: In Fresh Perspective* (Minneapolis: Fortress Press, 2005), although I am applying his argument differently than he does.

12. The wedding-marriage illustration is that one may privately tell one's beloved many times, "I am yours," or "I will be your husband/wife forever," or the like, and in Western culture one probably did just that. But that does not constitute marriage. One is married when one makes such a statement (perhaps a version that is far less colorful or intense than the one which has been made in private) in a defined format before witnesses. It is then that the officiant states, "I now pronounce you husband and wife" and signs the appropriate documents. And it is after that official pledge that everyone refers to the couple as being "married." Likewise baptism in the community of the followers of Jesus was the ceremony in which one pledged oneself officially to Jesus and His rule. It is only in the last 150 years or so that this has not been the case.

13. *Judgment* is a problematic word in the contemporary believing world partially because people do not understand its ancient meaning. In the contemporary world one comes into a court only if one is accused of a crime and thus the best that one can conceive of is a verdict of "innocent." But in the ancient world when a king came into a city or province he sat in judgment and would want his citizens or at least their leaders to all come before him. It is true that some would be those with whom he was not pleased and who would receive punishment, perhaps even execution, but it is just as true that, assuming that the city or province had not been in rebellion, many would be those with whom he was very pleased and they would receive his commendation, which might include a new title or office, a new honor, or a financial reward. That is a judgment that those who are faithfully serving His Royal Highness Jesus will eagerly await, since they long for His words, "Well done, good and faithful servant."

14. Mass evangelism, since at least Billy Graham, has tended to avoid the topic of baptism altogether because that was an end run on the issue of what to do with those who had been baptized as infants but either had grown up in families where there was no fervent commitment to Jesus so that they had not grown into such a commitment in stages or had rebelled against their family and its commitment until they attended the Billy Graham rally or InterVarsity group or whatever. The result has been that even some churches and denominations have tended to separate baptism and the initial act of commitment to Jesus, which makes it difficult for them to make sense of 1,800 years or so of church history (including many of the issues during the Reformation). It is as if the different traditions about weddings has been made optional, although perhaps important, extra so long as one could declare that one had made a private commitment to one another (especially if one could give the circumstances of that commitment).

15. Two works have influenced this language, the first being David J. Pawson in *The Normal Christian Birth: How to Give New Believers a Proper Start* (Hodder and Stoughton, 1989) and the second being Gordon T. Smith's *Beginning Well: Christian Conversion and Authentic Transformation* (Downers Grove, IL: InterVarsity Press, 2001). Both use the birth metaphor, especially Smith.

Chapter 12

How Do You
Move a Mountain
With a Small Shovel?

❧

Gary Best

Gary Best along with his wife, Joy, are the National Team Leaders of the Vineyard church family in Canada. He writes from a background of over 20 years of both traveling and teaching about the in-breaking Kingdom of God as well as putting that teaching into practice at a local church level. His great passion is to see "power ministry" spread from the stages into the life of every willing believer, and to experience the perfect double espresso.

THE SURPRISING PRAYERS OF THE NEW TESTAMENT

After more than 25 years of actively practicing prayer for others, I realize that I have learned a lot less than I first would have hoped. In fact, I am reasonably convinced of only two things. First, I am quite sure that prayer is not a system designed to make God do what He otherwise would be reluctant to do. ("Oh, they said the right words with the right inflection and volume, now I simply must do as they wish!") It seems to me that approaching prayer from this perspective is more likely to produce faith in results and/or methods than actual faith in God—the latter being the whole point of prayer.

Second, I suspect instead that prayer has more to do with changing us to become part of the answer to our prayer. It "tunes" our hearts so that we begin to pray and act in alignment with God's desires. As a result we are more prepared to join God in His work rather than trying to find a way to coax Him to support our agendas. The end result of prayer should be more submissive followers of Jesus.

The very response of Jesus when the disciples asked Him to show them how to pray seems to underscore this perspective. He encouraged them toward a constant and active expectancy— asking God to bring His rule to their own place and time: "May your Kingdom come soon. May your will be done on earth, as it is in heaven" (Matt. 6:10 NLT[1]). They were to believe that God would respond to this request. Then, following Jesus' example, they were to dedicate themselves to what they saw the Father doing (see John 5:19).

I must confess, however, that even a cursory reading of the Gospels seems (at least at first glance) to challenge this paradigm. Of course, most of the prayers Jesus and His disciples directed to God in private are not recorded; it is primarily the public prayers for others that we can read. Yet in these prayers at least, there is a boldness and directness that shocks us. They are less, "May Your kingdom come" and more, "Let it come now!"

Theirs are not complex prayers, difficult to remember. "See! Hear! Rise!" They are so direct and challenging that the only reasonable explanations for them are extreme audacity on the one hand or supreme confidence and faith on the other that God indeed desires and intends to perform exactly what they are demanding. They are prayers of Kingdom announcement, often spoken as though God Himself is uttering the commands.

KINGDOM ANNOUNCEMENT

We see this kind of announcement early in the Old Testament as Moses is sent by God back to Pharaoh's court. Moses was not unfamiliar with the power of Pharaoh: he had been brought up in privilege within the Egyptian ruling family. But any opportunity that might have been afforded by that background had, in Moses' eyes, been lost. He had long lived in exile, a wanted man, and had resigned himself to the life of a shepherd.

It is in this unlikely desert setting that God dramatically appears to Moses through an encounter with a burning bush (see Exod. 3). Intrigued by a bush that is burning yet does not seem to be consumed, Moses draws closer to examine this phenomenon; and as he does, God begins to speak.

What God shares with Moses is His will and intention for His captive people in Egypt. "I have certainly seen the oppression of My people in Egypt.... So I have come down to rescue them from the power of the Egyptians..." (Exod. 3:7-8). This must be the most wonderful news for Moses—news so wonderful it is almost too good to be true! What comes next brings him quickly back down to earth: "Now go, for I am sending you to Pharaoh. You must lead My people Israel out of Egypt" (Exod. 3:10).

If Moses had no prior experience of Pharaoh's court perhaps his response might be more enthusiastic. Instead, Moses knows all too well the odds against the success of such a venture. His reply is not unpredictable. "Here I am Lord, send my brother."

Nevertheless, given God's "persuasiveness," Moses and Aaron eventually find themselves in the very place where Moses feared ever to be: standing before the ruler of the nation of Egypt. Of course the battle is not simply a political one. This is a conflict between spiritual powers and principalities and Yahweh Himself with Moses and Aaron as God's emissaries. What do they announce? "This is what the Lord, the God of Israel, says: Let my people go . . . ." They are not appealing to God; He has already revealed His will to them. They are speaking from God and requiring obedience to His command.

Kingdom announcement.

This announcement foreshadows that of Jesus' later in the New Testament. As soon as He begins His Spirit-inaugurated mission, He announces, "The time promised by God has come at last . . . . The Kingdom of God is near! Repent of your sins and believe the Good News!" (Mark 1:15). To those who are enslaved and to those powers which enslave them He commands, "Let God's rule break in! Turn around and receive it!"

What gives Jesus such confidence to speak directly from God? Jesus knows that He has been sent from the Father at just this time for the very purpose of buying freedom for those who are bound, to reclaim them for the family of God (see Gal. 4:4). Second, He has a practice of constantly listening to His Father in order to understand where and how His mission is to be applied. In private He repeatedly prays the Kingdom prayer, "May Your kingdom come." Now, with the certainty that comes from that interaction with His Father, He announces to the needy crowds, "Let it come now!"

When His disciples express their astonishment at the authority in those kinds of prayers (even in unusual contexts), Jesus seems to encourage them to pray in the same way. "Have faith in God," He says. "I tell you the truth, you can say to this mountain, 'May you be lifted up and thrown into the sea,' and it will happen..." (Mark 11:22-23a). He then underscores for them the key to this kind of prayer: "But you must really believe it will happen and have no doubt in your heart" (Mark 11:23b). He is telling them that unreserved trust in and commitment to God's purposes can result in mountain moving faith—faith that produces the kinds of bold pronouncements they hear Him make.

PRAYING PRAYERS OF ANNOUNCEMENT

Many years ago, I experienced this gift of great faith in the midst of a very trying circumstance. Our only child to survive pregnancy was a strapping 2-pound boy we named Jonathan. Miraculously he had lived in spite of the odds, a credit far more to the mercy of God than to any faith on my part. Since the birth of our son, Joy had suffered two miscarriages and was within an hour of losing yet another baby. Consulting the doctor confirmed this fact. Finally (it was now in the middle of the night), I couldn't bear it any longer and retired to another room where I sadly began to pour out my anger toward God (Why do we always seem to treat our friends like our enemies?) because He had given us a number of promises for this little baby.

Surprisingly, in the middle of my self-justified tirade, God spoke to me from Scripture. In a sense, He simply asserted: "I said I would do it, and I will." This word came with spiritual force, hitting me in the chest like a hammer. A deep sense of peace and certainty came over me. I knew that God had declared His intentions. Without any premeditation, I began to speak to the plans of the devil for ill and I rebuked them, literally commanding the miscarriage to stop.

Some time after that I must have fallen asleep. All I know is that I woke with a start a few hours later, chiding myself for such lack of commitment and perseverance. I rushed into the next room to discover that God had stopped the miscarriage in its tracks. Our daughter Jaana is the delight of our lives today!

Very seldom, however, have I had such a strong confidence come upon me seemingly with very little effort on my part. I suspect that is true as well for most of us—these are infrequent events. I was certain that if I had this kind of experience again I would pray in the same way that I had in this circumstance. My difficulty was that I didn't know how to reproduce this visitation—it seemed entirely sovereign. As a result, my posture was a passive one—this certainly wasn't the kind of prayer that I was going to generate on my own! It would have to be initiated by God.

There was a variety of reasons for my hesitation. First of all there was simply the fear of failure. To speak to a blind eye and command it to see was in my view a very foolish thing to do unless you had a high degree of confidence in the result. (Didn't Jesus say we must really believe in our hearts that it will happen?) I remembered the story of Babe Ruth, the famous baseball player of the last century, who had the audacity before coming to the plate in a crucial "at bat" to point to the right field fence, indicating where he was going to deposit the ball. As the story goes, Babe then proceeded to hit a home run in precisely that place. To pray a prayer of command and not see the result would be paramount to calling for a home run before meekly striking out.

Second, to do so knowing that my percentages of success were realistically quite low (not to mention my doubt quotient being quite high) would seem to lack integrity. Lurking in the back of my mind in these situations would always be a strong measure of doubt. I certainly would have hope that God would be faithful, but to say unequivocally that He would definitely act seemed presumptuous. I was as worried about damaging God's reputation as I was my own.

Most of all, however, the main impediment that held me back from praying prayers of announcement was my fear for the wounding that such a prayer (if it proved ineffective) would inflict upon the person I was praying for. To command a sickness, oppression, or circumstance to change in a strong authoritative voice would most likely raise the hopes of the person being prayed for—if the prayer "failed" would not those hopes be dashed? Would failure undermine a foundation of hope and faith in them? Wouldn't it be safer to appeal to God on their behalf rather than to audaciously speak from Him? (I know people who had experienced that very thing and were devastated by it. Their hopes had been raised by the "certain" pronouncements of anointed people but the answers to their hopes had never come.)

Finally, I was personally hesitant because of some prayer "failures" of my own. Years after my experience of "mountain-moving" faith that resulted in the birth of our daughter, Joy and I received a visit in the middle of the night. Jaana, who was married and expecting her first child, was in danger of losing him. I prayed over her the same prayers of command that I had prayed over her mother. The words were the same, as was the authoritative voice; the result was not. I could not conjure up the faith that had come as a gift so many years before. I knew that this was not as simple as a system to be learned. Quite frankly, unless I was very convinced that God was taking the initiative, I was not going to experiment again.

Because of these reservations, my response to announcement prayers was a cautious one for many years. Yet at the same time I was always troubled by the noted absence of these faith statements in my life compared with the strong frequency of these prayers in the lives of Jesus' first disciples. My dilemma existed in how I was to get from where I was to where they seemed to be.

ANNOUNCEMENT IS PART OF A LARGER STRUGGLE

Interestingly enough, what helped me to break this impasse was an insight I received from a passage in J.R. Tolkien's book, *The Fellowship of the Ring*. In this story, the wizard Gandalf is standing at the end of a narrow stone bridge that spans a deep chasm. At the other end is an evil creature known as a Balrog. It is a classic depiction of a power encounter between good and evil. What struck me was how Gandalf responds to this evil threat. After establishing the nature of his authority, he boldly commands, "You shall not pass!" Here was a classic kingdom announcement!

What follows is not an immediate triumph, although it is ultimately Gandalf's survival that is an important key to the rest of the book(s). Indeed it appears at first that Gandalf does not survive, and it is only later that we discover that his bold words are simply the opening salvo in a life and death struggle. Gandalf's words are not a statement of arrogance or self-sufficiency; they are pronouncements of alignment. He is proclaiming that he stands for and with the cause of all that is good and right; he is declaring that ultimately because of the primacy of that goodness, evil will ultimately not triumph. Gandalf is not brashly saying that the evil creature has no chance of defeating him in the present encounter, nor that evil could not prevail for a significant period of time. He is saying that good will in the end overcome evil—on that confidence he makes his stand.

In this light I revisited the Kingdom announcements of Moses in the Old Testament and of Jesus and the disciples in the New. When Moses commands, "This is what the Lord says: Let them go!" there is no instant result. It is not the end of the conflict. In fact it is only the beginning. Pharaoh reflects for just a moment before responding, "No! In fact double their work load!" Moses' command simply serves to precipitate a series of power encounters that are a necessary part in Pharaoh's ultimate defeat. (See Exodus 5–11.)

At first the spiritual powers that undergird Pharaoh's realm are able to respond to the challenge of God's displays of power. When Aaron throws down his staff and it becomes a snake, they do the same. The fact that Aaron's "snake" devours theirs doesn't seem to dampen their enthusiasm. When he then uses his now restored staff to fill the river with blood, they (having retrieved their backup staffs) duplicate the feat. This apparently is intended to convince Pharaoh that all is well and that there is no need to relent in his stance. (I have always struggled to understand how increasing the measure of a catastrophe is seen as a solution but apparently they and Pharaoh took some comfort in that.) The same scenario is repeated with frogs with a similar result: Surprise! More frogs! This continues with a plague of gnats. Crestfallen, Pharaoh's magicians are forced to concede. "We can't do gnats. This is the finger of God."

The conflicts then continue from flies to livestock to boils, hail, locusts, darkness, and then eventually, to the death of the firstborn of both animals and people. Of course this sequence is not just happenstance: God is confronting the pantheon of gods from which the Egyptian empire has grounded its strength. The conclusion is unmistakable. Yahweh is King over all kings and rulers both physical and spiritual.

The encounters that comprise this conflict are marked by both actions and words. Repeatedly Moses and Aaron speak the same words of announcement, "This is what the Lord says: Let My people go!" Speaking out God's intention is simply part of the overall battle.

Jesus is God's own Son with unlimited authority. It is through this second person of the Trinity that the worlds are created with a word. Every demon who encounters Him in the Gospel accounts turns and attempts to flee. Demonic power has no hold on Him. It is not surprising then that He can simply speak a word of command and spiritually induced afflictions are removed and the person restored. Yet when even Jesus says, "Turn around and believe this Good News" many do not turn. He says, "Follow me" and many turn away. His prayers of announcement and command are tangible ways of saying, "Let the rule of God break in today and let it continue to break in until 'the whole world has now become the Kingdom of our Lord...'" (see Rev. 11:15). He is very aware, though, that between the first announcements and the final fulfilment will be many battles, not the least His own death.

FACING FEARS

As I began to understand this, I realized that it was essential for me to face my fears—both fears of failure and of disappointment—and contend for God's rule in the lives of people both with actions and with words. After the loss of two more children during pregnancy, our daughter conceived once again. The medical position was that she would not carry this child to full term. My emotional response was to simply run away or at least to keep my expectations manageable. The last thing I wanted to do was raise my hopes by pronouncing a positive outcome. Yet I was convinced for a variety of reasons that God did want Jaana to have a child. Certainly it was in line with His general will as revealed in Jesus. But I also felt like He had assured me that He would exert that will in her case.

Thus began months of waking each morning with a battle cry on my lips, "Let the will of God be done this morning! Here in this situation, in Jaana's body!" I never had faith beyond the day; in fact numerous times during the day I was drawn back to the same announcement: "Let the rule of God be done right now!" I can't say I ever had the deep-seated confidence that I had received as a gift during Joy's pregnancy with Jaana but I fought to reach it every day. This made the joy all the sweeter when Eden Jemimah was born.

As I persevered in planting and watering the small seed of faith I had, God was faithful in causing it to grow. I came out of that experience with a greater desire to contend for the will of God overcoming the rule of evil. For years I had hoped for a delivery van to simply back up and drop off fully formed gifts of mountain-moving faith. Now I was beginning to realize that I was responsible to nurture the seedlings I had already received.

Since then, when I pray for needs in the lives of others, if I believe that I know what God's will is in the situation, I simply ask them, "Can I fight for you in this?" I then explain what I believe God's desire to be for their circumstance. I also share with them how

I will pray: that I will address the sickness or the spiritual power behind it and announce that God's will is something different and that it must fall in line with His purpose and will. I am also very honest. I explain that I cannot guarantee that the result we hope for will indeed take place but that we will battle for it together. I explain that any boldness or strength in my language is an outcome of wanting to fully embrace whatever faith God is giving me for this and not a result of confidence in either a system of prayer or in my own abilities.

CAN WE KNOW WHAT GOD WANTS?

In all of this, we simply want to "do what the Father is doing" (John 5:19) just as Jesus did. As mentioned previously, though, not all faith comes to us in a fully mature expression, nor does revelation. The reality, as Paul reminds us in First Corinthians 13:12, is that we hear imperfectly and cannot always be absolutely sure that what we think we have heard is unmistakably God. This uncertainty is what makes the quest for faith the journey that it is. Like Abraham and Sarah, we must step toward what we believe God has shown us, even though at times we have little idea where that is leading.

How do we grow in our ability to discern when God has really spoken and when it is just our imagination? The author of Hebrews suggests that a major aspect of growing in discernment has to do with taking what we believe is the good and right thing and acting on it. He describes the mature as those "...who by constant use have trained themselves to distinguish good from evil" (Heb. 5:14 NIV). The heroes of the faith (see Heb. 11) said and did what they heard. If we want to move beyond simply being legends in our own minds, we must do the same. Only by doing what we hear can we grow in true discernment.

So whenever I pray for others, I ask this question of the outcome that we are praying for: "Is this something that is generally part of the will of God as revealed in the teaching and life of Jesus?" If the answer is no, then I am on shaky ground to "pronounce" at all. If the answer is yes, then I look for a secondary indication that God is affirming it now. Has God given revelation about the need or about His intended solution? Has He given me an inner confirmation that He does want to me to pray with this kind of authority (to move from "May Your kingdom come" to "Let it come")? Finally are there signs of the Holy Spirit's activity in the prayer activity; is He demonstrating visibly that He is at work? All of these things help me have a stronger sense of God's will in the situation.

Could I be wrong in my discernment of God's will? Of course I can. That is why it is so important to practice listening in the context of a mature community of other believers and within a lifestyle of being immersed in study of the Scriptures and of the lives of saints that have gone before us. Yet, as I have already emphasized, we can never arrive at mature discernment without being willing to act upon what we have already heard. Once we believe God has spoken to us, we need to battle relentlessly for that promise to become reality by speaking and walking it out. Double-mindedness is the enemy of faith. While it is helpful and important to evaluate the fruit of our hearing from God, if we do so too quickly, we will be paralyzed by indecision. The rule I follow is this: If I believe God has given me some direction, it will take a stronger, clearer "word" from God to cause me to question what I heard at first.

FINDING OUR VOICE

We all long for experiences where we are filled with such faith that we have absolutely no doubt about an answer to our prayer. This is what Jesus tells us is possible in Mark 11. How then do we grow in this? Some believe that the key is a system: if we speak the right words, God must respond. Others are convinced that the secret is in the tone or volume of our voice. Still others reject both of these suggestions. As a result we have a polarization of views and practices: some using prayers of command as a methodology almost assuming that God wants done what we want done, and others never venturing beyond general prayers asking God to do what He thinks is best.

While I suspect the validity of a system that puts us in charge of God, I do have great confidence that God wants us to find our voice to pray these prayers of faith. Of course all spiritual gifts are just that—gifts, not something that we can develop, master, or earn. Yet at the same time we can position ourselves with respect to His grace so that it can grow in us.

Practically what does this mean with respect to prayers of command? I believe that we can strengthen our voices (overcoming our fears and hesitation and growing in our belief and confidence) by simply using them. We must be willing to speak out that which we believe is God's will even if at times it seems like that belief is the size of a mustard seed. As we do, one of two things will happen. Either we will become increasingly convinced that this is indeed God's desire and we will speak it out with growing confidence, or we will become less and less convinced that this is God's intention at all. Both ways discernment grows and with discernment comes confidence to speak. We find our voice by using our voice.

FIND YOUR VOICE BY USING IT

My favorite character in the family film, *The Princess Bride*, is the drunken Inigo Montoya. For his entire life he has trained himself in swordplay to avenge the life of his father. Near the climax of the movie, he finally encounters the murderer of his father, a man with six fingers. A chase ensues only to result in Montoya being badly wounded by a dagger thrown by the six-fingered man (in complete disregard, one might add, for the accepted ethics governing chases of this sort).

As Montoya slumps defeated against the wall, the six-fingered man berates him for coming so close to the completion of his life mission only to fail so completely. He then reaches with his sword to plunge it through the heart of Montoya and end his miserable existence. At that precise moment, however, something deep within Inigo stirs—it is a revelation that he has not come this far only to fail. At the last moment he finds the strength to counter the thrust of the six-fingered man's sword so that it simply pierces his shoulder.

What comes from Montoya's mouth is barely above a whisper. "You killed my father; prepare to die." This of course enrages the six-fingered man who immediately attempts to stop this pronouncement once and for all. Again the sword thrusts toward the heart only to be deflected again. "You killed my father; prepare to die." This time the voice is spoken with greater intensity and conviction as though something is strengthening Inigo's heart and resolve in spite of his physical wounding.

Again the six-fingered man lunges; again Montoya's sword deflects the blow. This time he springs into action, filled with faith and passionate intensity. "You killed my father—prepare to die!" He found his voice by using his voice.

I am not, of course, recommending that positive thinking and speaking can produce the prayers of the New Testament any more than I am suggesting that avenging a life by taking a life is God's best answer. But I am saying that if God has placed a seed of faith in our hearts, it will grow as we commit ourselves to the truth of it by both word and action. And we will experience the truth of Jesus' words: "Keep asking, and you will receive what you ask for. Keep on seeking, and you will find. Keep on knocking, and the door will be opened to you (Matt. 7:7).

Central to our life mission as followers of Jesus is joining with him in "releasing the captives" (see Luke 4:18) by helping connect people with the in-breaking rule of God. We participate in this divine rescue in a variety of ways. One of the most powerful things we can do is simply trust and submit to God's kingship ourselves. This provides a living example and tangible "taste" of what God's rule looks like for those who embrace it. It can plant a seed of hope in those who are bound for the possibility of true freedom.

We can also actively bring this hope within the reach of those who need it by living out the Good News: praying for the sick, driving out demonic powers, loving unconditionally, contending for justice, and stewarding the environment that was given to our care originally in the garden. As St. Francis encouraged, our gospel should be one of action and not simply words.

But we must understand that battling with our words is also centrally important. We must proclaim our stand with God against the spiritual forces that oppose His will—once we believe we know God's heart and intention, pronouncing it boldly—by aligning our words with His. So we must certainly pray daily the prayer that Jesus gave us: "May your Kingdom come soon. May your will be done on earth as it is in heaven" (Matt. 6:10).

As we gain confidence that we know what it is that God's will is in the here and now, then we are to turn those words out toward God's enemy and announce, "Let His Kingdom and rule come now! Let the will of God be done!" Our words may begin as a whisper, but if we persevere, God will strengthen them with the authority of His own voice.

ENDNOTE

1. Unless otherwise noted, Scripture references in this chapter are from the New Living Translation of the Bible.

ABOUT THE COMPILER

FRANK DECENSO JR. has been engaged in teaching the Bible and theological subjects since the mid-1980s. His venues have been churches, home groups and Bible studies, and online forums.

He is also the author of *Presence Powered Living: Building a Life of Intimacy and Partnership with God.*

Frank and his wife of 16 years, Denise, attend Joy Vineyard Fellowship in Virginia Beach, Virginia.

ABOUT THE CONTRIBUTORS

BILL AND BRENDA (BENI) JOHNSON are the Senior Pastors of Bethel Church in Redding, California. Bill is a fifth generation pastor with a rich heritage in the things of the Spirit. Together they serve a growing number of churches that have partnered for revival. This apostolic network has crossed denominational lines in building relationships that enable church leaders to walk in both purity and power.

RANDY CLARK was used of God to birth the "Toronto Blessing" in 1994. From 1994-2004 Randy focused on leading renewal meetings throughout the United States and around the world. He is founder of Global Awakening, through which he conducts his international and national ministry. Randy and his wife, DeAnne, are parents to Josh, Tonya, Johannah, Josiah, and Jeremiah.

CAROL WIMBER is the wife of John Wimber, founder of the Vineyard Movement. They were married 42 years before his passing in 1997. Carol and John worked together in much of the birth and growth in the Vineyard. Carol is the author of *The Way it Was*, the story behind the man, and how the Vineyard came about. She resides in Yorba Linda, California.

CHRISTY WIMBER has been involved with the Vineyard Movement since the beginning. She and her husband, Sean, oversee DTS [Doin the Stuff] which handles John Wimber materials as well as others in the Vineyard Movement. Christy teaches at various conferences and retreats throughout the world. In 2006 she and Sean planted a new church, the Yorba Linda Vineyard, in California. They have two children, Camie Rose and John Richard.

S.J. HILL is a gifted teacher in the Body of Christ with over 37 years of experience in the ministry. He has traveled extensively, pastored, and has been on the faculty of Brownsville Revival School of Ministry. He has also taught at Mike Bickle's Forerunner School of Ministry. He is currently teaching part-time at F.I.R.E. School of Ministry in Concord, North Carolina. S.J. has also authored four books: *Burning Desire; Enjoying God; Personal Revival,* and *God's Covenant of Healing.*

BOBBY CONNER has an extensive ministry background as a Southern Baptist pastor and he ministers in a high level, proven prophetic anointing. He believes his calling is to equip the Body of Christ to hear and discern God's voice in these times. Highly esteemed as an internationally acclaimed conference speaker, Bobby has ministered to over 45 foreign countries as well in the United States. Bobby and his wife, Carolyn, live in Moravian Falls, N.C. They have two sons and daughter-in-loves and three grandsons.

DOUG ADDISON is the founder of InLight Connection and is the author of *Prophecy, Dreams, and Evangelism* and his latest project, *Accelerating Into Your Life's Purpose*. He travels worldwide helping people transform their lives and discover their purpose. Doug is a stand-up comedian and his training seminars include hearing God, understanding dreams and visions, and experiencing the supernatural. Doug also trains and leads dream teams and prophetic/power evangelism outreaches.

While attending college, **DAVID TOMBERLIN** had a dramatic encounter with the Holy Spirit that forever changed his life. Since that time, the Lord began to use David, and he has had the privilege of leading many to Christ. By God's grace, David has traveled to over 30 countries and ministers the Word of God with miracles, signs and wonders following. Originally from Texas, David currently lives in Southern California with his wife and daughter.

CHARLES H. KRAFT is on the faculty of the School of Intercultural Studies, Fuller Theological Seminary where he serves as Professor of Anthropology and Intercultural Communication. He holds degrees from Wheaton College, Ashland Theological Seminary, and Hartford Seminary Foundation (Ph.D. anthropological linguistics). He is the author of 29 books and numerous articles in the fields of missiology, anthropology, communication, inner healing and deliverance, spiritual warfare, and African languages and linguistics. Dr. Kraft is an ordained minister of the Brethren Church. He is married and has four children and twelve grandchildren.

MARCUS LAWSON is the founder of North Gate Church and Mighty Warrior Ministries. He and his wife, Linda, have spent 28 years in full-time ministry. Marc's passion is to see a revolution come to the western church as believers realize God is not restricted to moving only in services but as saints live out this supernatural lifestyle in their homes, at work, school, and in the marketplace! Marc is the author of *It's The End of the Church As We Know It— The 166 Factor*. Marc and his wife have five children and seven grandchildren and live in Woodstock, Georgia.

DENNY CLINE and his wife, Ann, have pastored in Oregon for 20 years. With a team of 27 adults, they planted the Albany Vineyard in 1994, where Denny continues to serve as senior pastor. They have been privileged to experience several awesome visitations of the Holy Spirit, impacting youth and adults alike with healing, salvation, and deliverance. It is Denny and Ann's dream to see thousands of people become carriers of God's glory to their neighbors, work places, and the nations.

PETER H. DAVIDS graduated from Wheaton College, Trinity Evangelical Divinity School, and University of Manchester. He is ordained in the Episcopal Church and has worked for seminaries of several denominations as well as served a variety of churches. He is presently Professor of Biblical Theology at the trans-denominational St. Stephen's University in New Brunswick, Canada, as well as a theological advisor for the German-speaking Vineyard movement, having previously served on its board. He has been married for 40 years to Judith, and they have three children and five grandchildren.

GARY BEST along with his wife, Joy, are the National Team Leaders of the Vineyard church family in Canada. He writes from a background of over 20 years of both traveling and teaching about the in-breaking Kingdom of God as well as putting that teaching into practice at a local church level. His great passion is to see "power ministry" spread from the stages into the life of every willing believer—and to experience the perfect double espresso.

Additional copies of this book and other book titles from DESTINY IMAGE are available at your local bookstore.

Call toll-free: 1-800-722-6774.

Send a request for a catalog to:

Destiny Image₍ₐ₎ Publishers, Inc.

P.O. Box 310
Shippensburg, PA 17257-0310

"Speaking to the Purposes of God for this Generation and for the Generations to Come."

For a complete list of our titles, visit us at www.destinyimage.com.